THE TELEVISION WRITER

The

Television

Writer

BY ERIK BARNOUW

HILL AND WANG ‿ NEW YORK

FIRST EDITION APRIL 1962

Manufactured in the United States of America
by American Book–Stratford Press

for K. B.

Preface

To writers, television offers forms and techniques of astonishing variety. In these pages I have tried, among other things, to explore and survey this diversity. A major section of the book, Part 2, "Techniques and Practices," provides illustration by means of brief, annotated excerpts from fifty-three television scripts of recent years, representing varied lines of development in filmed, taped, and live television.

But the writer in television is involved not only in a medium but also in an industry. Books on television writing have largely avoided this problem, merely advising the writer that he must, of course, adjust himself to the realities of current markets. But we know by now what this means: it means writing one-hour dramas one year, retooling the next to write quiz material, then switching to Westerns, then to crime dramas. This book takes a different view. It suggests that television will become a really meaningful medium for writers (and audiences) when writers take a larger role in shaping their working environment. Literary currents in the novel and the theatre are made by writers: in television, writers bob helplessly, adjusting as they go. In time, the television writer must assume a role of leadership in his medium.

All this should begin with an interest in problems in which writers were, until recently, encouraged to take no interest whatever. That is why Part 1, "The World of the Television Writer," which seeks to provide a frame of reference, deals not only with the medium but also with the web of conflicting forces at work in the television industry of the United States, and with the writer's role—and potential role—in relation to them. This is new territory for a book of this sort and I am well aware that the problems raised call for much additional thought and study.

Part 3, "A Business Portfolio," returns to various specific aspects of the television writer's relationship to his complex industrial environment.

I want to thank Harper & Brothers for their courtesy in permitting inclusion of material previously appearing in *Writer's Roundtable,* edited by Helen Hull and Michael Drury. My deep thanks also to Evelyn Burkey, Richard Jablow, Ashbrook Bryant, Gretchen Burkhalter, Marguerite Cannavaro and numerous television writers, for their valued help on specific points.

E. B.

Contents

Preface, vii

1. The World of the Television Writer, 1

2. Techniques and Practices, 47

3. A Business Portfolio, 159

Selected Readings, 171

Index, 175

THE TELEVISION WRITER

1. The World of the Television Writer

1. The World of the Television Writer

MIDWAY through the twentieth century oblong luminous screens appeared suddenly in numbers of homes. From city streets you could see them glowing in the interiors, with small, shadowy figures moving in the bright oblong. Briefly considered a plaything of the rich, the screens became almost at once a fixture in tenement and shack. Quickly adopted by taverns, they were also soon installed in schoolrooms. First a monopoly of industrial powers, they speedily made their appearance also in underdeveloped countries. Soon they were established on every continent, and thousands of writers throughout the world were writing for the luminous screen.

For writers the little screens represented an astonishing new channel to the attention of millions of people. Notions about its power spread rapidly, rooted in case histories: (1) in America a little-known politician, after a few appearances on the small screen, was considered a major presidential candidate; (2) a little-known lipstick became almost overnight a national leader in its field, increasing its sales by several thousand per cent through television sponsorship.* What unguessed powers lay in the small screen?

Hundreds of thousands of scripts have been written for television. While its masterpieces may lie in the future, achievements to date give a firm basis for analysis of the writer's role in it. What forms has the television writer evolved? What tools

---

* Chester and Garrison, *Television and Radio*. References are more completely identified in the bibliography, p. 173.

3

are available to him? What limitations face him? What markets invite him? What is his place in the growing hierarchies of television? Much of what we shall have to say will apply wherever the small screen continues its historic penetration; some of it will be applicable mainly in the United States, since every nation develops its own patterns of organization and control, reflecting its economic system and power groupings.

In every age the forms used by the dramatic storyteller have reflected many things: to begin with, the physical nature of his stage. Thus, the Elizabethan dramatists, writing for a "scaffold" without scenery, were under no strong pressure to consolidate their action into a limited number of scenes in a limited number of places. They therefore tended to begin a story at its beginning and to let it move freely through time and place. Nothing deterred Shakespeare from leaping from Alexandria to Messina to Rome to Athens, from palace to street to galley to battlefield, often using scores of characters and a lot of physical action en route. On occasion a narrator might be used. On the bare platform he did not seem out of place. All in all, a story could take its natural course. This usually resulted in an early point of attack, many characters, many scenes, and a loose narrative structure.

As the theatre subsequently became involved with background painters and eventually box sets with doors, windows, ceilings, furniture, knickknacks, crockery, food, fireplaces, and legions of technicians, the writer came under constantly increasing pressure to stop moving around so much, with a result that he necessarily concentrated on the later parts of his story. He now discovered, more and more, that the unities of time, place, and action held some attractions of their own. It became axiomatic that he must introduce his characters as *already involved* in the problem that would be resolved by the climax of the play. On the way to the climax we would somehow learn what had led to the problem—never through a narrator, who is unwelcome in a box set, but mainly through retrospective dialogue.

The writer now had to be ingenious about finding occasions and reasons for his characters to talk about the past. This, it often turned out, could be done most conveniently in a living room or a solarium. The usual result of all this included a late point of attack, few characters, few settings, emphasis on indoor drama, avoidance of physical action, and an exposition often continuing in small doses throughout the entire play. In a typical Ibsen last act we are still learning about things that happened twenty years before.

One kind of television is directly descended, via the Broadway theatre, from this Ibsen tradition. We mean the television plays of Paddy Chayefsky, Reginald Rose, Gore Vidal, and others, written for live series like the Philco-Goodyear *Playhouse,* and therefore, under circumstances that pushed toward compression and unity. Thus we find that every Chayefsky play begins at a point where the characters are already deeply involved in the problem with which we are to be concerned. On a restricted canvas, usually within hours or days, we find the problem unfold. Rose tells us, "I try to keep my television plays moving in the shortest time span I possibly can . . . I have never written a television play which covers a time span of more than three days. . . ." *

In a sense television gave a new opportunity to this kind of modern drama. Such drama depends more on character than on action, and for this purpose the television screen is a magnificent instrument. Where else can an audience, at a distance of a few feet, observe the minutest twitch or flicker? Also, the play of limited scenery need have no sense of restriction. Television cameras can be constantly on the prowl, showing us always new vistas and juxtapositions even within a single room. Objects and details of settings can swim into view at strategic moments, entering and leaving the spotlight like characters. They are no longer mere static backdrops to action. And television can, even within a single set, handle time more flexibly than the theatre can—as we shall see.

All this helped Chayefsky and others put new life into the tightly constructed, late-attack play. His work was, in fact, so impressive that some books hold this the *only* kind of television to be urged on writers. But, of course, many people in television

* A. S. Burack, *Television Plays for Writers.*

have always chafed against it, including those who came to television from the world of film and brought with them very different habits and traditions.

Early in this century film people were already finding that their future lay not in drama resembling the products of the stage, but in something quite different. Finding that film could jump easily from Alexandria to Rome to Athens, from tavern to canyon to ranch, they began to burst free of the unities of time and place and action. Physical action, instead of being avoided, began to be sought. The late point of attack no longer held attraction, especially if an early attack made it possible to introduce a stagecoach robbery, a cattle stampede, a roof-top chase, a battle, or other alarms and excursions. If the Ibsen theatre drove the dramatist indoors into living rooms and all-purpose solaria, film drove him outdoors again. In the United States it drove him to the open spaces of southern California. It drove him also back to a fluid, multiscene structure. These are the traditions and habits that film people brought to television. If live television has had Ibsen in its blood, filmed television—*Cheyenne, Lassie, Hong Kong, Hawaiian Eye*—has tended to be Shakespearean, at least in structure.

Of course, the two traditions are no longer quite so neatly separable. In television they have tended to influence each other, each imitating the other's successes. Film-television people have often seemed as intent on proving that they too can do the Chayefsky sort of thing as live-television people have been to prove that they can do Westerns or naval battles in a studio. The development of studio equipment and particularly the coming of videotape recording have made it easier for them to do so, lessening the pressure toward consolidation. *Playhouse 90* was more mobile than the earlier Philco-Goodyear *Playhouse*. Still, one notes the rival traditions pulling the writer in opposing directions.

Our discussion of two major traditions has been an oversimplification in another way too. Still other traditions enter the picture. Television is a medium not only of entertainment but also of journalism. Some television drama is a little of each, in form and in content. Sometimes, in television, entertainment and journalism are so involved in each other's affairs that we are not sure which is which.

Of course, this kind of journalistic involvement is not new. John Fletcher and Philip Massinger, in *Sir John Van Olden Barnavelt* (1619), dramatized the exciting news of the hour. Written at top speed, the work was apparently rushed into production on the heels of the events portrayed. But theatre, for many reasons, has not generally welcomed such ventures, and journalism was virtually a monopoly of print when film, and then broadcasting, began to lure it into other spheres.

Today, in television, dramatist and journalist live in close association, belong to the same union (the Writers Guild of America), use the same techniques, and have overlapping functions. In simplest form, television journalism is narration, with or without news footage or news pictures. The interview, which television has used with enormous flexibility, is also important to it. But the television journalist has moved into interpretive and background programs that sometimes use staged scenes and re-enactments.

The rationale for this is clear enough. Is the truth confined to what chanced to happen in front of a camera? Since a word-report is necessarily a kind of reconstruction, why not also pictorial reconstructions? And so the television journalist asks the little girl to go back into the house and come out again, schoolbooks in hand, just as she did before the angry women began to scream at her—in order that he may get it on film and intercut it with newsreel footage of the screaming women. He asks the visiting statesman to go back into the plane and come out again, so that the historic handshake can be photographed from a better angle. "Sometimes I don't know," said a newswriter at a Guild meeting, "whether I am a journalist or a dramatist." Adhering to truth as he knew it, was he not a journalist? Since he also had a hand in the events before the camera, was he not a creative artist, a dramatist?

When Edward R. Murrow and Fred W. Friendly, of CBS, undertook to present a report on an important civic controversy in Indianapolis, they had their staff film the separate meetings of the two groups that were principally involved, the American

Civil Liberties Union and the American Legion. Excerpts from the two meetings were then arranged in a rapid alternation, giving the effect of a grand, historic debate. It was brilliant television, probably journalism, and certainly a work of creative drama.*

If television journalism has taken on aspects of dramaturgy, television drama has shown a corresponding tendency to take on the guise of news documentary. Sometimes one hardly knows which is which.

A fiction-drama series, Armstrong *Circle Theatre,* decided, after a period of ever-dwindling ratings, on a change of policy. All programs would be based on recent news stories. But the programs continued to be acted by actors and their dialogue to be written by writers. Many scenes were not easy to distinguish from scenes in fiction plays. As if to proclaim their truth, the producers brought in a prominent newscaster as narrator. The result was fiction-type drama in a newscast framework.

Dragnet similarly used the form of a report, a case report by a "policeman." Besides narrating, he appeared in the action. The content in this case was "based on" the files of the Los Angeles police department. The dialogue was writer-invented and not from files. Was it fact or fiction?

The shadowiness of the dividing line holds fascinating implications which need not detain us at the moment, although they are worth pondering. Our point now is that television drama, trying to exploit journalistic values and to convey an up-to-date and inside-information feeling, has made wide use of the narrator, a figure virtually banished from drama until rehabilitated by radio and then television. In television, filmed, taped or live, he appears as a real or fictional newscaster, reporter, policeman, private detective, warden, minister, nurse, secretary, or sometimes nameless entity. He may be seen, or unseen, or sometimes seen and sometimes unseen. He may speak from an identified place or no place, from a fixed point in time or no time, or from various places at various times. The fixed point in time, if there

* "Incident in Indianapolis," in Murrow and Friendly, *See It Now.*

is one, may be after the end of the story, or it may be before its climax, with the final scene following the final narration. The narrator may be addressing no one in particular, or the television audience, or an intermediary who may be seen or unseen, heard or unheard. The narrator's identity may be clear to us at the start or may for dramatic reasons be withheld until later. The nature of the place from which he is talking may be made clear to us at once or concealed until later.

The variations and combinations of variations are endless. Of course, most of these are available also to the writer of the printed page. They seem worth mentioning here because narration has not, in Broadway theatre or in film, been thought a normal tool of drama. The writer of plays, wrote Kenneth Macgowan as late as 1951, in *A Primer of Playwriting,* "must convey everything through the dialogue of living men and women." Broadway thought this and so did Hollywood. Despite the Greeks' and Shakespeare's "choruses" and occasional modern deviations, narration was not considered acceptable. In film, before television, it was for newsreels and travelogues and not normally for the story film.

The use of a narrator in the long top-ranking *Dragnet* series, and in others of similar pattern, had led to play constructions quite different from anything in modern theatre or film tradition. An episode of *Dragnet* might have a number of dialogue scenes, largely indoor scenes, scattered throughout the play. Alternating with these would be rapid-action sequences, including indoor and outdoor action, usually photographed silently but used with narration, music, and often sound effects. Production convenience and economy have contributed to this development.

The rise of the narrator, especially the visible narrator, was undoubtedly encouraged by other factors besides those we have mentioned. The television advertiser needed pitchmen; audiences therefore quickly got used to being talked at from the luminous screen as had seldom been done from the large screen. Then there were, on various drama series, "hosts" and "hostesses"— a generally superfluous role devised to add name value, and to lure well-known performers into being salesmen. Then, too, there were the comedians. If the American theatre has, by and large, preferred to ignore the audience, this was not true of vaudeville and night club. Talking to an audience was natural to Jimmy Durante and Bob Hope. George Burns, cigar in hand, transferred his monologues to television with ease, and made them a narration linking acted episodes. In a memorable drama series Herb Shriner did likewise, establishing a surrealistic atmosphere in which he could interrupt scenes, discuss situations with the characters as well as the audience, then permit them to continue, then interrupt for another commercial. These informal patterns, reminiscent of cabaret or summer camp, seemed magnificently applicable to the intimate screen.

A special television invention is the spontaneous narration, obtained via interview. NBC's one-hour drama *The Story of a Family* concerned an actual family in the Southwest. It was performed in the Robert Flaherty tradition, by the people themselves. Crises in the family saga were re-enacted. But narration was also used. Early in the production process the mother was encouraged to talk at length, before the camera, about her family. This material was not used in interview form, but segments of what she said were used as narration at various points.

In fact, in this play the same technique was used with all members of the family. This made it possible at various points to introduce a scene with a quick succession of brief comments by *various* members of the family about the coming episode. This kind of drama, with its alternation of dramatic episodes and multiple narrations, recalled in its structure neither Ibsen nor Shakespeare, but possibly Sophocles—with a chorus of Texas women!

We have suggested that the interaction of different traditions and functions has been fruitful for the television writer, widening his range of activity and technique. He is sometimes entertainer, sometimes journalist, sometimes publicist, sometimes not sure which. But he is other things too—sometimes teacher.

From this notion many television executives will shrink with horror. But obviously, big-audience, commercial television teaches, even as it entertains or informs. The teacher traditionally has a hard time competing with entertainment and even journalism, but there is food for thought in the experience of television. Among the experiments of the *Omnibus* series, the most popular have been those built around great teachers, educational in form and content: a series dramatizing the origins of the Constitution, with a great lawyer as narrator; a series on the historic Adams family, with a leading historian as narrator; a history of the dance, with a celebrated choreographer narrating; a series of expositions on classical music, with an important conductor and his orchestra. All these made use of any tools of drama that television could provide, but the dominating figure in each was a narrator appearing not just as a reporter but frankly as an educator.

Curiously, these successful experiments are additional examples of television returning to earlier dramatic forms and functions. Pre-Elizabethan religious drama was also frankly a teaching drama.

But there are still other developments, important to the television writer and his range of techniques, that must be mentioned. There is, for example, the drama peopled not by the living but by creations of the artist. We shall have to use the term *animation*. To many people this suggests rabbits, mice, and extravaganzas of sadism. To those in the field it has a broader meaning. Including cartoon and puppetry, it can include other resources of the graphic and plastic arts. Some have become important in television.

It took television a long time to become interested in animation. Although old cartoons showed amazing durability on the small screen, animation was almost ignored as a source for new programming. It was considered too costly; and executives tended to think of it as a children's medium—as Hollywood had, of course, taught them to do. Walt Disney made an early entrance into television, but he used it mainly to promote theatrical film properties.

Television's first solid encouragement to animation came in the field of commercials. How a combination of ingredients stops the hammer in one's brain, how a pill dissolves in the stomach, how an exclusive ingredient bounces away tooth-decay germs, how a filter refines away harsh flavor—these were matters that animation could show easily in an eight-second spot. Commercials also contributed some brilliant new animation characters, such as the Piel brothers.

Presently television documentary producers also began to turn to animation for sequences like animated maps, flow charts, cross sections, pie charts, bar charts. To demonstrate the invisible, the abstract, the too-large, the too-small, animation could be invaluable. In another of the scrambling actions fostered by television, documentary writers and animation writers became more and more involved in each other's business.

But animation producers were interested in more than commercials and demonstration sequences. They wanted a place in the main spotlight; they wanted to produce series telecast in the peak hours of maximum viewing. The breakthrough came about 1960. *The Flintstones,* a half-hour drama series in animation, was scheduled in midevening and was soon near the top in program ratings. It brought a boom in half-hour animated drama, and it brought new writers into the animation field.

A characteristic of animation is its absolute control over time. The live-action dramatist accommodates himself to the normal pace of human movement and muscles. But in animation, actions that might normally take minutes, hours or days, can be done in a split second if the dramatist wishes. Over him, time exercises no tyranny; it is his plaything.

The Flintstones avoided the zany pace of some animation but still managed to cover, in each half-hour episode, dramatic plotting that would take hours in other media. The medium also allowed an escape from the literalness that too often hamstrings television drama. Its characters, extravagant but human, could dwell simultaneously in prehistoric and modern times, so that a family cave could be equipped with television, a bullock cart with a cigarette lighter. Speed and absurdity gave it a primitive satisfaction, but it managed to combine this with fairly adult satire—a rare ingredient in television—so that it appealed to different audiences on different levels, and seemed to open new vistas for the television writer.

But while animation was enjoying a television vogue, it was

also in a state of inner conflict, which the writer needs to understand.

From its earliest days animation has assumed that the reconstruction of motion is the indispensable glory of the medium. In synthesizing motion, animators have felt, they took a step forward from the still arts, in which motion is merely suggested by being caught in mid-air. But is it really true that the Discobolus would be more exciting if he would just throw that disc? Do people keep looking at Mona Lisa *in spite* of the fact that her smile is frozen in time and place?

In recent years restive animation people have persistently experimented in a simplification of their medium. Instead of synthesizing motion, with the requirement of innumerable drawings, they provide an element of motion in other ways: largely by movement of the camera *in relation to* the art. Thus the camera moves *in* toward a significant detail, or moves *out* from a detail to the whole, or *across* from one portion to another. Or sometimes one pictorial element moves across another.

In this way, in a notable experiment, Abe Liss produced for CBS-TV the film *Hook,* which told the story of a hawk by means of two hundred special drawings by Hazard Durfee and a script adapted from a story of Walter van Tilburg Clark. There was constant movement. Wheeling and zooming over Durfee's craggy landscape, one had a hawk's-eye view of the world. One zoomed with him toward his prey. One saw the wounded bird in the underbrush, then looked with him toward the tops of trees. Pictures and action were brilliantly complemented by a musical score by Carlos Surinach.

If the producers of *Hook* had busied themselves with a constant synthesizing of the flapping of wings, it would have required at least twenty-four pictures per second or some forty thousand pictures for a half-hour film—a standard animation quota. It would have required, too, that army of intermediate artists—animators, inbetweeners, inkers, and opaquers—that is brought into play in most animated productions and ultimately gives them a homogenized quality. This was true, for example, of *The Flintstones,* which used normal animation. The simplified animation or *camera animation* used in *Hook* not only eliminated these and reduced costs, but accomplished something more important: It brought the texture of Durfee's original drawings to the screen. In doing all this, the film posed important questions. Can animation escape from its factory atmosphere? Can it become a medium for individual expression, a new kind of collaboration of artist, writer, and composer?

Clearly, storytelling on television can be done via graphic artist as well as via actor, and *Hook* showed that the artist need not be a cartoonist. To both artist and writer it gave a glimpse of a new horizon.

Curiously, while animators were moving toward such new forms, so were others. And this is another example of the interplay of different groups and traditions in television.

At NBC-TV the Special Projects Unit had busied itself for a number of years with documentary films made from historical footage. Beginning with *Victory At Sea,* for which Richard Rodgers had composed the score, the unit had won new standing for a technique that, in the theatrical-film field, had always been treated with some disdain. After several projects of this sort, the unit decided to broaden its activity with another technique, also held in low regard by the film industry. Assembling thousands of photographs, drawings, engravings, paintings, and cartoons, of Abraham Lincoln and his period, the unit decided to make a history film with *camera animation.* Experimenters in various countries had been making films of this sort for years, but in spite of brilliant achievements such as the Canadian *City of Gold,* they were still regarded by most film and television leaders as a fringe group, producing for film societies or classrooms, not for large-audience entertainment.

Yet *Portrait of Lincoln* found a sponsor in the Lincoln Savings Bank and won so enthusiastic a response from audiences that it was at once earmarked as an annual television feature. It was followed by other, similar programs, including the memorable *The Real West.*

Philip Reisman, Jr., its free-lance writer, proposed this project to the NBC-TV unit, outlining a suggested structure and listing categories of pictures to be sought. A tentative script, indicating proposed style, was included. As pictures were found—in the National Archives, local historical societies, private collections, and NBC's own growing files—the script was completely rewritten to fit material found and to derive maximum value from it. The words written, sometimes biting, sometimes lyric, sometimes deeply moving, achieved a brilliant partnership with the pictures and music. Like a good musical score, the words did not slavishly underline the pictures but established a complementary rhythm of their own. Never a series of captions, they yet indirectly supplied the hints and facts needed to give full meaning and impact to the pictures. Occasionally, when the audience was sufficiently oriented to extract full value from a sequence of pictures without assistance, the script allowed music to "take it away," to replace words in the aural spotlight. In this type of film, as in films using historical or other silent-film footage, a writer sometimes achieves his finest moments when he lays the perfect groundwork for a climactic, wordless sequence.

A program of this sort, using archive material, is generally held together by narration, but it also can use dialogue. The material can be combined with new footage. The archive material is generally photographed on the equipment used in the animation field—an *animation stand*. On such a stand a camera is mounted face downward, on a shaft that permits it to move up or down. The table below it, on which the artwork is placed, can move east to west or north to south or can rotate, or use a combination of these motions. The stand can provide minutely computed, perfectly controlled movement of camera in relation to artwork, and it is, therefore, invaluable to a program like *The Real West*.

But what should we call this medium? Is it drama, journalism, education, animation? The boundaries of such words grow fuzzy in the face of a program of this sort. The film had an impact like that of *The Covered Wagon* of silent-film days, or *The Grapes of Wrath* of the sound-film era. While the form of its sound track was largely narrative and its pictures came from archives, and while its technical work was done on an animation stand, yet its impact was essentially that of drama in any meaningful sense of the word. The past lived again before us and we were part of it.

Here again we have a picture of the television writer in the midst of conflicting currents and enriched by them. The 1950's, the first full decade of television, were a period of production ferment and experiment. Traditions long unchallenged in other media came together in a new arena. The result, for the writer, was a broadening of his function and of the range of technique. Television was exciting because it did not, like theatre and theatrical film, settle down to a narrow range of activity, forms, and functions. There was opportunity. Writers, among others, responded to it.

Perhaps these words seem puzzling to a television viewer of the 1960's. He looks at program listings and asks, "What happened?" He might, in 1961, find a single night's schedule offering him *Tombstone Territory, Rescue 8, Malibu Run, Wagon Train, Hong Kong, Wanted—Dead or Alive, M Squad, Hawaiian Eye, Sergeant Dekker, Trackdown, The Californians, Naked City, Johnny Midnight,* and only a sprinkling of other kinds of programming. All this reminds us that the television writer works not only in a medium but in an industry. To define his problems we must look not only at his techniques but at his professional environment and relationships. These too are part of the world of the television writer.

This is a story with disturbing elements. It has to do with what has been called the "industrialization of the writer."

Our founding fathers attached importance to the role of the writer in society, and in the Constitution they provided special protection for him. It gave Congress the right

> to promote the Progress of Science and useful Arts, by securing for limited Times to Authors and Inventors the exclusive Right to their respective Writings and Discoveries.

The language and intent are clear. The founding fathers wanted to nurture the arts and promote the flow of knowledge and ideas, and they apparently felt this could be done by strengthening the position of the author. Therefore they empowered Congress to enact copyright legislation which would secure control over published material to the author. With respect to writings, only *authors* are mentioned.

What happened to their intention makes a fascinating case study. In 1909, at the dawn of the new media of communication, Congress passed a new copyright law theoretically based on the constitutional clause. In actuality it neatly reversed the meaning of the clause. By legislative edict, it simply changed the meaning of the word "author." The law states:

> the word "author" shall include an employer in the case of works made for hire.

Thus the company, the corporation, began its career as author, becoming the heir to those blessings which the founding fathers had earmarked for authors. Congress had said to the corporation, "You too can be a successful author."

Now of course there was a grain of logic in all this. In a sense, creation in the new media has become a group undertaking, often a corporate undertaking. But to assume that the group creation replaces individual creation is to make a fatal error. For anything of significance to be set in motion, a lonely man still has to think and work with pencil or typewriter. The completion of his work may later require legions of other workers, but they come to little without his act of creation. He may be writer-director or writer-producer or simply writer; he is still needed.

The new law gave the rising new media a special incentive to deal with writers as employees. The film industry early acquired a preference for employee-writers, as did radio. And "employee" soon came to include free-lance writers, even many who worked at home on their own initiative.

In the early years of radio a writer who had placed a script occasionally found that the check by which he was paid carried such words as "in full payment for my employment as writer of . . ." In endorsing the check, he acknowledged an employee status. When contracts were used, they were often framed in employer-employee terms: the writer was considered a tem-

porary employee during preparation of the program. During
that time he was expected to be available for revisions.

From the company point of view, a virtue of dealing with
writers as employees was that it settled without further discussion all matters of ownership and control. The company as
"author" owned all rights, in the absence of any agreement to
the contrary. The early writer in the broadcasting field almost
never received air credit, was not paid for rebroadcasts, and did
not share in subsidiary rights. Revisions were made without his
consent and even without his knowledge. Scripts could be made
to mean the opposite of what the writer intended, and sometimes
they were. The writer could be barred from rehearsal, and on
many series he was, as a matter of policy. It was precisely as if
the founding fathers had written:

> Congress shall have Power to deprive Authors of all Right
> to their respective Writings.

The early efforts of radio writers to improve their status often
consisted of protesting agreements couched in employer-employee terms. Some writers liked to insist, "We're independent
contractors." But during the 1930's the passage of the National
Labor Relations Act introduced a new and ironic complication.

Offhand, nothing would seem duller than the question whether
a writer is an "employee" or an "independent contractor." And
in truth many writers were not in the least interested in the
issue. But it turned out to be of great importance to them.

The point was that, under the new labor law, employers were
obliged to bargain with their employees collectively about things
like wages and working conditions. But that was not true in
the case of independent contractors; in relation to them, the
same sort of collective bargaining might be a conspiracy in re-
straint of trade, a violation of the antitrust laws. For the free-
lance writers it meant: If we're employees, we may use our collective strength; if we are not, we may not.

Free-lance writers became more interested in being "employees" at about the same time that networks and sponsors
began to refer to them persistently as "independent contractors."

During the 1940's and 1950's the issue was gradually resolved. First the networks, then the independent producers, made firm collective-bargaining agreements with free-lance writers. These agreements state that they apply to all writers properly classified as employees and not to those who are not employees. Clearly the range and impact of the contracts depends on how *employee* is defined.

Today television writers, including free-lance writers, are covered by collective agreements negotiated by the Writers Guild of America with networks and other producers of live, taped, and filmed programs. In such a contract *employee* is defined in this way:

> *Persons covered.* This agreement shall cover freelance writers . . . rendering writing services as "employees" . . .

> An employee . . . shall be any writer . . . as to whom the company has the right by contract to direct the performance of personal services in making revisions . . .

In other words, the right to demand revisions became by definition, and logically so, the essence of an employer-employee relationship. And since apparently no advertising agency or network or other producer wants to give up the right to demand revisions, the result has been that virtually all free-lance writing for network television is today covered by the Guild agreements, and virtually all such writers *are* employees, including those who work at home. It includes work done on the writer's own initiative. The writer submits an outline if he is established, a draft if he is not. If the company is interested, a contract is signed under which he becomes an employee until completion of the production. The employment may be temporary and part-time and may involve no specified working time or place, but it is employment none the less.

So employee status became the norm. What have been the results? For writers, beneficial results have been these: Through collective bargaining they have achieved enormously increased economic power. Collectively they have forced agreement to the principle that, at a stipulated time after a live telecast, essential rights revert to the employee—referred to, in some legal cases, as "the actual author." (Since a substantial number of television plays have become Broadway plays and Hollywood films, this is invaluable.) Foreign rights, book rights, have become important assets to writers. In the case of filmed programs, rebroadcasts are paid for and have become a rapidly mounting source of income. On live, filmed, or taped programs, air credit is required. Even its relative position and the relative size of its type are specified in the collective agreements. Indignities that were long standard practice have been removed. Rates of pay have been increased sharply.

But note one thing: The entire improvement, and the power that made it possible, rest on what is essentially the writer's servant status. This is the irony. The cornerstone of the writer's economic power, in television, is the one indignity most galling to him: lack of control over his writings. The employer can still demand revisions and even have them made by others. A play can still reach the air meaning the opposite of what the writer intended. Many writers demand an end to this and want their Guild to establish for the writer "moral rights" in his work—particularly the right to prevent others from tampering with it. But such a right would, it seems, automatically take him from under the umbrella of labor law and deprive him of the right to bargain collectively. This is the major irony in the status of television writers. They are powerful, but their power rests on that status into which they were nudged by copyright law and lured still further by labor law—employee status. Before embracing this status they were impotent. Now they are strong, except where many of them would most like to be.

Can the writer move forward from this point? Perhaps, though not through labor law. Meanwhile, one thing should be clear. If the writer is to be, in almost all cases, an employee, with all that this implies, a crucial question is, Whose employee? If his work is to be controlled by others, the question of who will do this controlling will be all-important. And this will be true not only for the writer but for the public, whose right of access to a diversity of views is at stake.

Let us look, then, at who employs, who controls the writer.

In the complexity of television there are at least six kinds of employer. Let us look at them one by one.

The first employer is the television station. In the early days of television, stations gave substantial employment to writers. Many stations launched local drama series. Almost all local production of this sort has vanished. Some stations have almost abandoned studio production and rely on network offerings, films or tapes from other sources, and sports. Some add local news and interviews. For these, many stations maintain one or more staff writers, who may also have other duties. More ambitious local programming has become rare. At the several dozen noncommercial stations, locally produced programs are often substantial in number, but due to lack of funds, of facilities, and of personnel, they are largely ad-lib lectures and discussions; only occasionally have they become a field for the writer. For him, the station—commercial or noncommercial—has become an arid land.

There are exceptions. The series *Play of the Week,* which featured originals as well as adaptations of important plays, was a television station project. But its production anticipated revenue from distribution to stations in other cities, via videotape, and it must therefore be thought of as a *syndicated* series. It will be mentioned again when we consider program syndicates as employers of writers. Syndication is one way in which stations can remain active forces in programming despite rising production costs.

The television station operates in the legal framework developed in the Radio Act of 1927 and revised in the Communications Act of 1934 and later amendments. The word "radio" in the law now means television as well as radio.

A basic premise of the law is that the broadcasting channels are a precious resource belonging to the people. In these publicly owned channels, the Federal Communications Commission has the duty of deciding "the composition of the traffic." A television station must have a license from the Commission. The license is for a limited period, not more than three years. The station acquires no property right in the channel. At three-year intervals it must apply for renewals. The renewal is supposed to depend on whether the station is serving the "public interest, convenience, and necessity." License transfers have to be approved by the Commission.

Because the range of broadcasting frequencies available to television is limited, the allocation of channels was early felt to have important implications. The Commission decided that no television licensee should be permitted to operate more than five stations in the VHF (Very High Frequency) wave band that includes channels 2 to 13. And no licensee would be granted more than one such channel in any one area. The Commission was determined to prevent any concentration of power that might limit the range of subjects and ideas available to the public. America's television licenses were therefore divided among a large number and variety of licensees. The Commission has aimed at "diversity" in their allocation. Such policies are naturally of interest to writers. But, as we shall see, their effect has been almost entirely negated by other factors, especially in recent years.

The American system of broadcasting gives the individual television station broad powers and responsibilities, and a sweeping freedom to carry them out. The law *forbids* the Federal Communications Commission from censoring the station. The station, throughout its license period, is responsible for programming decisions. On the other hand, at renewal time the Commission has the responsibility of deciding whether the station has served the "public interest, convenience and necessity," and of granting or denying the renewal accordingly.

The system was splendidly conceived but has aspects of peculiar unreality. At the time it was taking shape in congressional committee, in the mid-1920's, the national networks did not yet exist, and the assumption was that stations would themselves be the program production centers. Thus it seemed logical to make the station responsible for what it broadcasts. In theory the station is still responsible. In theory it cannot divest itself of this responsibility. In actuality the network-affiliated station has long ago relinquished effective control over major time periods, including the evening hours that matter most. In practice the station has not even seen a large proportion of what it broadcasts. Thus, the control system has become largely a myth. Under these circumstances license renewals have tended to become automatic; it has seemed illogical to punish a station for sins of others over whom it has no control.

If the station has relinquished powers which it had in theory no right to relinquish, why was this permitted? It was permitted because the implications were not at once clear, and because the advent of network broadcasting was clearly a necessity. The pattern envisaged in the law was obsolete by the time the law was passed. Network broadcasting was needed. And although its development has involved many conflicts and problems and has made the Commission's job an almost impossible one in the framework of present law, it did represent an essential step.

With this preamble, let us consider the network as an employer of writers—setting aside for the moment the problem of its ambiguous status.

The network is essentially a web of contracts. An entrepreneur negotiates with a group of stations agreements that will enable them to operate at times as a unit, usually via connecting cable. The contractual device on which American networks were built was the *option*. The entrepreneur, the "network," was given an option to buy, for resale to national advertisers, specified time periods on all stations in the group. The option enabled the network to sell time to a national advertiser coast to coast, in one transaction. Previously an advertiser would have to negotiate separately with each station.

The cables that carry programs from one station to another are not owned by the network; special telephone company cables are leased. And the network does not necessarily own stations; one leading radio network, Mutual Broadcasting System, has owned no stations. However, each of the major television networks has found it advisable to acquire five VHF stations (the maximum permitted by law to any licensee) in different broadcasting areas.

Each of these networks is, of course, a licensee as to the few stations it owns, but not as to its network operation. Whatever supervision the Commission exercises over network broadcasting must be exercised through its power to license stations and to attach reasonable conditions to the station licenses.

The network shares with the stations the revenue from network time sales. The usual allocation gives the networks at least two thirds of the revenue and divides the remainder among the stations. Under this division the station receives less for time sold to a national advertiser through the network, than for comparable time sold directly to a local advertiser. But the arrangement gives the station prestige programming from New York, Hollywood, Washington, and other centers, on all continents. This increases the value of the time reserved for local sale. The system is thus lucrative for station and network alike. The Commission, concerned that licensees were yielding control, has imposed various restrictions on the option clause. But the mutual advantages to station and network—as well as to national advertisers—have kept the system in full force.

Network affiliation has tended to affect television station operation in the following way: portions of the station's schedule, including the most valuable evening hours, are yielded for network use and call for little attention from its own staff. Other periods, reserved as station time, may be sold to local or regional advertisers. Some of this time too may be sold through the network to national advertisers, if the station wishes and the opportunity arises. There are still other alternatives, as we shall see presently. While the station staff is more concerned with the programming in station time than with that in network time, we shall see that a growing proportion of programming in station time also tends to come from the large metropolitan centers.

The network performs for the station another service not yet mentioned: it fills unsold time periods with "sustaining" programs. During the early years of television, as during the dominance of radio, much network time remained unsold. The network has always used some of these periods for "public service" programming. The sustaining-program schedule has therefore provided an important element of balance in that it has included programs that have not usually interested advertisers. Over the years, network achievements in this category have been impressive. They have included opera, symphony, classical drama, documentaries, public affairs, experimental drama. Network enterprise has, in time, won advertiser support for some programs of this sort. Witness occasional sponsored programs of symphony, Shakespearean drama, Greek drama, and series like *Twentieth Century, Victory At Sea,* and *CBS Reports.*

For the television writer all this has been important. He has come to look to the network for two kinds of employment: (1) on commercially sponsored programs, often of fairly standardized sorts; (2) on programs of a more challenging or experimental nature, designed to give the schedule over-all balance and diversity and to develop programming that might eventually attract commercial sponsors.

Not many years ago, programming in the second category occupied many of the best viewing hours. In recent years, to the dismay of many viewers as well as of many writers, such programming has been swept to the fringes of the program schedule. Thus, the *CBS Workshop,* which brought to public attention work of Orson Welles, Norman Corwin, Archibald MacLeish, Jerome Lawrence, and Robert E. Lee, was broadcast in a midevening period throughout its radio history and for a time in its television history. But when last telecast it was scheduled on Sundays at noon, Eastern Standard Time, which in Western areas meant early Sunday morning, a time of minimum viewing. An experimental program without an audience serves little purpose. Writer contributions to the series were a disappointment to CBS, as was inevitable. The once great prestige of the series was dissipated and it was soon canceled. All this was part of a trend that has dismayed writers and has driven many to other media. We shall return to this problem presently.

Meanwhile, it should be noticed that both in commercial programming and in public-service programming the networks have shared the spotlight with other companies, other employers of writers. Their relations with the networks must be considered in some detail. But first let us look at each of them separately.

The advertising agency became active as producer and employer of writers in the earliest days of radio network history. The first problem of the networks was to obtain a share of the advertising appropriations of major corporations. For this purpose they offered all recognized advertising agencies the same commissions on the sale of time as they had generally received from magazines and newspapers on the sale of space. This commission, 15 per cent, remains the standard. If an advertising agency purchases on behalf of General Motors a series of weekly one-hour television network periods at $100,000 per week, the advertising agency receives from the network a commission of $15,000 per week. This transaction refers only to the time charges. The sponsor will have additional charges for technical facilities and also the cost of the program: writers, performers, designers, musicians, directors, executive producers, as well as scenery, royalties and other production expenses.

In the days of radio and the early days of television it was often the advertising agency itself that engaged the talent and coordinated the program; the agency "produced" the program. It billed the production expenditures to the advertiser, generally with a 15 per cent commission added. Thus the agency has generally received commissions on both program and time charges. The program commission is usually comparable to the time commission.

In radio the advertising agency became the leading force in commercial programming, but in the television era it has tended to withdraw from active producing and to assume a program-supervising role. The complexity of television, the large number of people needed to co-ordinate even a single series, the rise in overhead costs, led the advertising agencies increasingly to contract with others to administer the production—either the network itself or an independent producer, whose role we shall discuss in a moment.

Advertising agencies have had some distinguished television programming to their credit. *Kraft Playhouse,* for example, was produced by the advertising agency J. Walter Thompson. But by and large, the advertising agency as employer of writers has not had a glorious history. Its business is advertising and its sole preoccupation is service to the advertiser. The agency's substantial commissions depend entirely on the advertiser's decisions. The agency has always been inclined to discuss a play script as though it were copy for an advertisement. The famous decision to remove all mention of gas chambers from *The Nuremberg Trials,* in deference to the public-utility sponsor of the program, would not seem at all strange in the atmosphere of an advertising agency. There have been countless episodes of this sort, amusing and horrifying. But it is a mistake to exaggerate their importance. At most agencies the Nuremberg trials would never have been considered a suitable subject for a program, a suitable backdrop for a commercial, and therefore would never have been discussed.

The tragedy of the advertising agency's role in programming must be sought not in incidents of this sort, not in scripts censored, not in scripts rejected, but in scripts never written, subjects never considered. At the advertising agency self-censorship has tended to become a part of everyone's automatic process. Its executives vie with one another to save the sponsor from alleged perils. The writer as an employee of advertising agencies is likely to find himself surrounded by people who regard as perfectly normal the resulting zeal for self-censorship. The writer may even begin to doubt the validity of his own yearning for more meaningful material. The advertising agency's gradual withdrawal from producing is not to be regretted. But it does not mean that its role has ended, as we shall see.

The independent producer appears to have entered the picture as a program contractor working under supervision of the advertising agency. A television example is provided by *Circle Theatre.* Produced for some years by the advertising agency Batten, Barton, Durstine & Osborn, it was then handed over to an independent producer, Talent Associates. Batten, Barton, Durstine & Osborn remained in the picture, supervising.

The independent producer is not in the advertising business and receives no network time commissions. His concern is with the program, which he produces as a contractor. He is usually paid a per-program lump sum, a "package" price, which presumably covers program costs plus a profit. On some series the package price is the same for each program although costs may vary. On other series the package price is determined separately for each program on a cost-plus-percentage basis. The advertising agency usually adds its own commission to the package price and, of course, continues to receive its network time commissions. The arrangement places the advertising agency in a detached position of control. Besides supervising the program, it plans and supervises the production of the commercials, which may involve another independent producer.

Independent producers originate many series, submitting proposals to networks as well as to advertising agencies. A contract usually requires approval of network, agency, and sponsor.

For the writer, working for an independent producer is often preferable to working for an advertising agency. He is at least working for a specialist in television rather than in advertising. A producer of strength and prestige may be able to protect his employees from the more foolish whims of sponsors and their agents.

On the other hand, the writer working for an independent producer may find himself merely working for various employers simultaneously. On the *U.S. Steel Hour,* for example, a writer may find himself in a script conference with representatives of the Theatre Guild as independent producer, Batten, Barton, Durstine & Osborn as advertising agency, United States Steel as sponsor, and CBS-TV as network, all discussing problems of script revision in a kind of summit conference. "I attended," writes Rod Serling about *Noon on Doomsday,* which was telecast on this series, "at least two meetings a day for over a week, taking down notes as to what had to be changed." Such meetings may continue even in the final week of rehearsal. Film production, especially on location, does not seem to lend itself as conveniently to this kind of day-to-day supervision, but it seems to lead to still greater caution in the planning.

Successful independent producers have had a variety of backgrounds. The Theatre Guild brought to television its distinguished theatre background. Time Inc., independent producer of some brilliant *Close-Up* documentaries sponsored by Bell & Howell, brought a journalism and film background. A branch of the Ford Foundation first developed the *Omnibus* series as a sort of television "workshop." Harvey Comics, a leading publisher of comic books, became an independent producer in television with *Funday Funnies*. The entry of various major film studios into television has been in the role of independent producer, as with Warner Brothers as producer of *Cheyenne*. The variety of the backgrounds of these producers has contributed to the diversity of television.

However, the related interests of some independent producers raise disturbing questions, especially for the writer.

A talent representation firm, serving as agent for a roster of star performers, directors, and writers, is in a strong position to become an independent producer. Instead of offering its clients as individual artists, it builds "packages," aiming at the profits of an independent producer. Some of the largest talent representation firms have put together large numbers of network series, either owning them or administering them on behalf of other owners. The writer may thus find that his agent has become his employer. When this happens, the agent-employer generally does not deduct the standard agent's 10 per cent from the fees he pays the writer. But the arrangement still poses a problem.

The writer may be especially attracted to an agent who can also employ him. But an agent is supposed to win for his client the best terms obtainable in regard to fees and rights. An employer, on the other hand, has an interest in obtaining talent as economically as possible and in retaining maximum control of rights. A clear conflict of interest is involved when the agent is also the employer. It is questionable whether this is a legitimate combination of activities.

Somewhat similar problems arise in connection with another kind of independent producer, the network itself.

In the early days of network broadcasting, the network was mainly a producer of sustaining programs. The production of commercially sponsored programs was for many years the almost exclusive province of advertising agencies, supplemented by independent producers, who gradually rose in prominence. During this period the network contented itself with profits made from the sale of time. But in the 1940's each network made a determined and partly successful effort to develop packages for commercial sale. When such a sale was made, the network usually earned not only revenue from the sale of time but also the profit of an independent producer. One of the network's hopes in pushing this policy was to find advertiser support for public-service programs which it felt it had to maintain for program balance—although many network-built packages clearly have had no relation to this purpose.

The advent of television gave the network an opportunity to pursue its goal with substantial success. Technical knowledge was, at first, scarce. The network itself had behind it a period of production experimentation and was therefore in an ideal position to make sales of network-owned, network-produced programs along with time sales. Some of the most distinguished commercially sponsored packages have been network productions. They have included Philco-Goodyear *Playhouse, Wide, Wide World, Playhouse 90, See It Now, Twentieth Century, Victory At Sea,* and a substantial number of spectaculars.

Distinguished as this roster is, the role of the network as package producer has created issues. The network holds an option on the most desirable hours on stations coast to coast, which are in turn licensed by the Federal Communications Commission to serve the public interest. Although the station theoretically cannot divest itself of its responsibility, the network regards itself as inheriting the station's responsibilities as to the hours the network takes over. To do otherwise would no doubt place the entire system in jeopardy. Thus the network is an unofficial gatekeeper standing across the main entrance to the best time on publicly owned channels. Among the programs and sponsors clamoring for the choicest hours it must make its selections in the public interest. This would be a heavy task for the wisest. But the network makes it heavier when it puts itself in the position of choosing between programs in which it has a financial stake and others in which it has no stake.

This problem becomes thornier when we consider the coproduction. An independent producer plans a series of films for commercial sponsorship and places its plans before the network.

It offers the network a partnership in the project. The network invests in the project and becomes part owner; it will share in all future revenue, whether from network use or syndication or foreign use. A pilot film is produced. In negotiations with advertising agencies and sponsors about possible time periods and programs, the series is discussed. The series wins a sponsor. It goes into a valued time-slot. What was the relation between this culminating event and the coproduction arrangement? To rival independent producers, who may have seen no need to invite a network into partnership, the arrangement has a devious look, not unlike the kind of arrangement in which a disk-jockey is a consultant to a record company. Certainly there is a conflict of interest between the network as gatekeeper and the network as shareholder.

There are still other kinds of independent producer. There is the star who, with retinue, turns into a corporation and wins substantial tax advantages. He incidentally becomes an employer of writers, an editor. Some actor-producers have proved brilliant editors, while some show more interest in the enlargement of roles and egos. Still another kind of independent producer is the writer himself. In forming and controlling a package he too has tax advantages. He has, in addition, the incentive of acquiring a fuller control over the final form of his work. But his success in this respect may depend on his relations with advertising agency, sponsor, and network.

There are also packages in which numerous partners have a financial stake: agent-producer, star, director, writer, network, and others.

It will be seen that the writer in television is surrounded by a tangle of conflicting interests. Hundreds of pilot scripts are written, hundreds of pilot films produced. Is it always the most valuable and vital that reach the promised land of prime evening time? Before we go further into that question and try to chart a course for the writer through the jungle, we must turn to another employer of writers, the syndicate.

The syndicate, already mentioned, is modeled after the feature syndicates of the newspaper field. It produces series on film or tape and makes them available to stations for local use. Generally operating from Hollywood or New York, the syndicate offers the television station programming comparable to network programming, which the station can offer to local or regional advertisers, or to a national advertiser who wants to increase his efforts in some areas, or who cannot secure network time to his liking. The rise of the syndicate has intensified the decline of local programming and made the programs sponsored by national and local advertisers remarkably alike in form and content.

The rates paid for local use of a series vary with the size of the community. Use in Dubuque costs less than use in Philadelphia. Use is generally exclusive in the area, for a limited period.

Because a successful series can be repeated many times and each time earn new fees, in hundreds of cities in the United States and abroad (some series, like *Sheena, Queen of the Jungle,* have had more than a dozen syndication reruns) the eventual profits can be enormous. Many syndicated series are translated for commercial use in Japan, Germany, and elsewhere.

On the other hand, the returns are often slow and the investment may be enormous. Twenty-six or thirty-nine programs must generally be produced before distribution of a series can begin. Ziv, a leading syndicate that merged with United Artists of the motion picture field, has generally invested $1,500,000 to $2,000,000 in the production and promotion of a series before its distribution starts. Failure of such a project means heavy losses.

Factors that make for failure are many. The most galling of all, to syndicators, is the existence of *network time.* By what right, says the syndicate, do networks have this hold on the choicest hours on hundreds of stations? Syndicators are among those who like to point out the dubious legal standing of network option time. If the offerings of syndicates could more readily break into the favored hours, they consider that their sales would mount rapidly. Hemmed into station time, and competing for that time with a growing backlog of syndicated series of earlier years offered for rerun at bargain rates, the syndicators are inclined to pessimism, or indignation.

Meanwhile, the networks, already involved in network operation and package production, compete with the syndicates through syndication departments of their own. Among the offerings of these departments are network programs of previous seasons: *Victory At Sea* has been in syndication almost continuously since its first network use. The networks also have a special variation of syndication: via cable in station time, they offer series which the station can use to serve local advertisers. Time is left for the local commercials. *Meet the Press* is an example of a network-produced series offered in this way for local sponsorship, in a network equivalent of syndication.

Thus syndication has become increasingly competitive, involving hard struggle for slow returns through many small sales. Network programming, in contrast, offers the possibility of quick returns through a single sponsorship contract. It is not surprising that the syndicate, before launching a series in syndication, may try first to place it as an independently produced network series under sponsorship of a national advertiser.

The syndicate as an employer of writers reflects the uncertainties of syndication. Since everything must be produced before anything is broadcast, audience reaction will be unknown until the total investment has been made. The syndicate, above all producers, is inclined to seize on a formula in which it has confidence and stick to it. The thirty-nine programs of a syndicated series are likely to be thirty-nine variations on what is regarded as a reliable formula. If this is not likely to lead to experimentation, caution is further encouraged by the large number and variety of advertisers who will have to be satisfied by it: a brewer in one city, a department store in another, a creamery in another, a bank in another. A dispute over an alleged lapse of taste or a supposed political implication may entail the soothing of not one disturbed advertiser but seventy-five disturbed advertisers. To the syndicator anything controversial means not one headache but seventy-five headaches. The syndicator, conditioned by his way of life, is perhaps the most cautious, the most formula-bound employer of writers; at least, he has been, to date.

If challenging material goes into syndication, it is usually after network or local use. We have mentioned *Play of the*

Week. This station production was videotaped. Sponsored in the New York City area by Standard Oil of New Jersey, it was then offered for syndication in other cities. The difficulty was that the plays ran approximately two hours. In New York, in evening time on an independent station, they attracted attention as an adult alternative to a network schedule dominated by formula series—Western, crime, and family. Few other cities had non-network stations on which this pattern could be applied. Few network stations had time to accommodate *Play of the Week* in suitable hours. The station-time hours available were either half-hour periods or fringe periods. The memorable *Play of the Week* therefore had a somewhat disappointing career in commercial syndication. Much of its subsequent distribution was to noncommercial stations through the National Educational Television and Radio Center, to which we shall return presently.

In the tug of war over the precious hours of television, one employer of writers has not yet been mentioned: the public-service agency. In this term we include governmental agencies and private, nonprofit educational and religious organizations.

Both networks and stations have made it a practice to give time, occasionally or regularly, to agencies of this sort. The agencies are usually expected to pay the program costs, although these are sometimes shared with network or station. The agencies can seldom pay for time, although there are cases in which they do so.

Programming provided by agencies of this sort has included some of the most vigorous work done for television. Scripts written by Morton Wishengrad for the *Eternal Light* television programs of the Jewish Theological Seminary are among the most adult written for the medium. Universities, health agencies, welfare agencies, and museums, too, have produced fine programming—the series *What in the World* was a television milestone. Important contributions have been made also by the National Educational Television and Radio Center, which was launched with the aid of a Ford Foundation grant to provide programming, on an annual fee basis, to the noncommercial television stations. In areas not covered by such stations the programs are offered to commercial stations, for sustaining use.

Outstanding series have included *Casals Master Class,* winner of a Venice Film Festival award.

In earlier years commercial stations often gave evening periods to programs of public-service agencies but in recent years have relegated these increasingly to fringe periods of minimum viewing. The incentive to organizations to invest in such programs and to artists and writers to participate in them has therefore declined sharply. This is one of the most serious of current danger signs.

Station, network, advertising agency, independent producer, syndicate, public-service agency—these are the employers of the writer. On their intricate relationships, rivalries, arrangements, and deals, fortunes may depend. The power of the medium, the varied rewards it can bestow, perhaps make it inevitable that a tug of war should exist. Throughout the 1950's it seemed to be leading television through bold exploration toward a shining future. Then, within a short time, it seemed to be leading to disaster. Diversity was vanishing; series after series was a carbon copy. Crime formula, cowboy formula dominated almost all schedules.

It was especially catastrophic for the future of the medium that the "anthology series" seemed in danger of disappearing. A series of this sort, exemplified by Philco-Goodyear *Playhouse,* invites writer contributions without specification of required character, locale, or formula. The play is the thing. It is cast according to its needs. Anthology series enriched television with works of Paddy Chayefsky, Gore Vidal, Horton Foote, Reginald Rose, Robert Alan Aurthur. Writers responded to the open invitation of these series in a way that gave television for some years the initiative among dramatic media and made it the mecca of young writers and a major source for other media. In a handful of years anthology series were the wellspring of such stage plays and feature films as *The Miracle Worker, Twelve Angry Men, Marty, Visit to a Small Planet, Patterns, Bachelor Party, The Tenth Man, Requiem for a Heavyweight, A Catered Affair.* Now the door apparently was being closed on most of such activity. Instead came series that did *not* say to the writer, "Write us a play." They said, "Write us a vehicle for _____ _____ in the role of a private eye named _____ _____."

Final act should have strong action sequence. Study our formula before making submissions. Submit outlines through recognized agents."

That there was advantage to star-producers and agent-producers in such series was clear enough. Network and sponsor, too, saw advantages: name value, apparent assurance of tested formula, freedom from controversial matter. But the long-run risk to television was incalculable. Suddenly there was no reason for any new writer to turn to television. To writers of substance, new or established, the invitation to write variations of a formula was an invitation to go elsewhere. Chayefsky, Vidal, Aurthur, Foote, Wishengrad turned elsewhere. Many writers who stayed did so because they had nowhere else to go. Required to write formula or nothing, their talents were tragically wasted and misused.

To television writers, who had generally taken for granted the business affairs of their medium, the situation was one of crisis. Seeing now the destruction of diversified programming, they began to speak up. At a hearing of the Federal Communications Commission in 1961 David Davidson, national chairman of the Writers Guild of America, said, "Never in history have so many writers been paid so much for writing so badly."

If many factors were involved in the deterioration—including the dominance of the star, the rise of the agent-producer, the attraction of the coproduction—most important in the eyes of many writers was the dominance of the advertiser. Balanced in earlier years by substantial evening-hour programs of other kinds, programs reflecting advertiser preference had come to pre-empt almost all desirable periods.

To some, this did not seem a problem. It did to writers. Many of them saw it as a dangerous concentration of control in one interest group.

Concentrations of power in the communication media are not new. In several instances they have brought government intervention. Monopolistic trends in communication media have been regarded as especially serious because they limit freedom of expression.

From 1909 to 1914 the motion-picture industry was controlled by the Motion Picture Patents Company. It was the pooling of a group of patents that gave this control. Theatres, in order to get projectors, accepted the conditions of the Patents Company. Producers, too, in order to get cameras, went along. The Patents Company decided that the standard length of a motion picture should be fifteen minutes. The idea of the feature film, the longer film, was in the air, but the controlling group considered it a troublesome innovation. Short films had for years been the staple of the industry, yielding good revenue, so the ruling group wished to continue with them. Fortunately, rebellion within the industry, plus government antitrust action, put an end to the dominance of the patent group. Though writers were hardly a force in the film industry at that time, they had a stake in that struggle. As the grip of the patents group was loosened, some of the most brilliant film innovators—including D. W. Griffith—were able to rise in the industry and make their contribution to it.

The 1940's brought another conflict over concentration of power in the film industry, culminating in the 1948 Supreme Court decision in *United States v. Paramount et al*. The mechanism which had in this instance enabled an inner group to exercise effective control was ownership of the principal theatres. A group of major film studios which co-operated closely with one another collectively owned 70 per cent of the first-run theatres in the ninety-two largest cities. This dominance enabled them to control other theatres through block-booking agreements; to get films from any studio in the group, such theatres generally had to take a year's output without right of choice. As a result of ownership and block booking, in 1943–44 eight companies received 94 per cent of all film rentals. Because of this firm control, new independent producers could have virtually no access to the market, except in a fringe of theatres outside the system. During the period of this dominance, foreign films had very limited opportunities in the United States. Foreign producers had occasional access as suppliers—never as competitors—of the controlling companies. The films that were assured of wide distribution were those that emanated from the Hollywood studios of the inner group. The censorship unit maintained by the group itself therefore exercised effective nationwide censorship. The tastes of the inner group, its aversion to anything controversial, its taboos on specific subjects, had the force of law.

The court ordered the studios to divest themselves of their theatres and to desist from block booking. Coming at the same time as the rise of television, the order caused far-reaching upheaval. At first its impact seemed purely destructive. But in the wake of reorganization, several hundred independent producers have entered the motion-picture field. Until 1948 the market would have been closed to them. Because big-studio censorship no longer controls the divorced theatres, a larger range of subject matter has reached the screen. Foreign films have entered in rising numbers, providing intellectual and artistic stimulus. Independent producers not tied to studio investments have increasingly produced films abroad, enlarging still further the range of film content. When the government brought suit against the inner group, many screen writers thought of it as a remote quarrel between government and the companies, over business practices. In due time they learned that they had had a great stake in the dispute.

In the middle 1950's the Federal Communications Commission appointed a study committee to analyze the business interrelationships involved in network broadcasting. It was headed by Dean Roscoe Barrow of the University of Cincinnati School of Law. The resulting Barrow Report, made public in 1957, startled the industry. It said that network option time involved a relinquishment of station responsibility to the networks. Moreover, it said, there was "at least a reasonable possibility" that the arrangement would be found a "*per se* violation" of antitrust law. The report compared the control achieved through option time to that existing in the film industry before the Paramount decision.

The Commission, disturbed, studied the opinion. It issued a regulation to stations, to the effect that option time clauses in affiliation agreements should not exceed two and one half hours in any six-hour period. Option time thus survived, but the report continued to be studied.

The situation might be summarized as follows: The Federal Communications Commission, to avert a concentration of influence, had limited licensees to five standard stations. Control was thus theoretically scattered among innumerable licensees. But the most desirable hours on the overwhelming majority of stations came to be programmed by three networks. So long as these maintained a semblance of program balance and diversity, the possible implications of the development were not apparent. In the years when much network time remained unsold, the implications were not apparent. But in later years, as network schedules tightened, the implications became clear. The networks, selling control of the air piecemeal to others, developed a situation which a Commission chairman has described as a "waste land." Controls vested by government in local stations had been allowed by networks to slip to others—mainly to the limited group of advertisers who can pay $200,000 an hour for television programs. Clearly these were remarkably alike in tastes, fears, attitudes.

To writers, this domination and the limits it places on freedom of expression are a crucial concern. For the same reason they are of governmental concern. In the Paramount case the Court said, "We have no doubt that moving pictures, like newspapers and radio, are included in the press whose freedom is guaranteed by the First Amendment." This factor, to the Court, made any trend toward monopoly especially serious. But, if it was serious in the film industry, it was clearly all the more so in an industry operating in publicly owned channels dedicated to the public interest.

To the extent that the Commission itself polices the *status quo* in television, preventing others from infringing on its licensees, it becomes itself a party to any one-group domination that it has allowed to develop. The Commission is very conscious of this as it pursues its study of the interrelationships of network programming, which have given such an air of unreality to our control system.

The Commission has reason to be perplexed and troubled. The implication of the Barrow report seems to be that option time should be banned entirely. Would this destroy the networks? This does not seem certain, but it is at least possible. And the networks, as the Commission knows, have been responsible for most of television's finest achievements.

The syndicates, on the other hand, would find their opportunity in the banning of option time. Have the syndicates made any contribution to television comparable to those of the networks? These are some of the complexities that confront the Commission as it studies the issues of control.

A premise of this book is that the television writer has a vital stake in governmental policy in this area. It is important that he understand the problems involved. It is also important that he present his views in any appropriate channel, whether legislative hearing, Commission hearing, broadcast discussion, or printed page.

The writer should not make the mistake of thinking that freedom of the press, which in the view of the Supreme Court includes broadcasting and film, was invented as a privilege for writers. It is important mainly because it is essential to an alert and informed public. But the public cannot readily know whether there is freedom of the press and the writer can. The writer must therefore be one of its main defenders. When limits are placed by any interest group on the range of permissible subject matter, it becomes his duty to say so.

The following pages outline a suggested platform and program for television writers. They are written not in the expectation that other television writers will agree, but in the hope that it will lead to a more searching discussion of the drift of television by writers and others.

That advertising might have a role in financing the use of our precious channels has been widely accepted since the early 1920's. At that time all spokesmen of broadcasting and of government insisted it should be a secondary role. It would be "unthinkable," said Herbert Hoover as Secretary of Commerce, to have the medium used for "direct advertising." The code proclaimed in the late 1920's by the National Association of Broadcasters, the trade organization of the broadcasting industry, said there should be no advertising between 7 and 11 P.M.*

The more prominent role that advertising has played need not surprise us. But the most serious step in this direction was

* Charles Siepmann, *Radio, Television, and Society.*

the readiness of the networks to give editorial control to advertisers and their agencies along with the sale of time. It is true that the networks have maintained a negative control; the advertiser's program selection has required the approval of the network, and the network has consistently added its own censorship to that of the advertiser and the advertising agency. But this multiplication of negatives has hardly added up to an editorial policy. By and large, the network has conceded that the general character of a series, its content, its point of view, are the domain of the advertiser and his agency. To this there is an important exception, to be discussed later.

The network has not merely conceded the right of advertisers to select and control; in general, its attitude has *encouraged* them to do so. In the early days of network broadcasting the networks persuaded advertisers that radio had a unique ingredient that was missing in other advertising media: a close association in the minds of the audience between the advertiser and a beloved program and its performers. The advertiser has thus been impelled to feel that there was an important unconscious relationship between product "image" and the nature of the sponsored series. Whatever truth there may have been in this, it made the advertising specialist an entertainment engineer as well as an image engineer and has tended to make our cultural life, insofar as broadcasting influences it, a by-product of merchandising. The very success of television in attracting the advertiser into an increasing number of periods has brought us face to face with the disastrous effect.

But though editorial control by the advertiser has been with us for some time, it should not be thought of as an essential part of the "American system of broadcasting." It was certainly not so thought of by any spokesman of any point of view who testified at hearings leading to the laws within which our television system operates. It should rather be thought of as a temporary distortion of the system. Advertisers' veto power over news stories was once considered a problem in the newspaper field, but it was never raised to the status of the "American system of journalism."

The view is often heard that advertisers will, in time, become educated to sponsor "better" things. Actually the advertiser is well aware of what he is doing and has generally behaved as other people would behave in his shoes. When an executive of a large corporation, responsible to a board of directors, is given a choice between two series costing about the same, one reaching 22 million viewers and the other reaching "only" 17 million viewers, it is foolish to expect that he will not favor the 22 million. Faced by an inquisitive board, pressed to explain his selection in terms of "cost per thousand viewers" or "cost per new user," could he justify any other decision? He may at the same time join a Parent-Teacher Association committee in his home community urging better television and feel he has made some contribution to progress, but at the office he reaches for the one decision that makes statistical sense. And so it happens that *Playhouse 90,* a program of large audience and high achievement, falls by the wayside in favor of a Western series, and another anthology series yields to a gangster series. Multiply this a few dozen times, one decision at a time, and you have program sequences like *Hong Kong—Hawaiian Eye—Naked City—Johnny Midnight—Racket Squad—Harbor Command—Code 3—Rough Riders—Aquanauts—Wanted, Dead or Alive —Wagon Train.**

The question is not whether advertisers in these circumstances have made decisions that are less than statesmanlike, but whether such decisions should have been put to them in the first place. The question is whether the public interest is achieved by this piecemeal auctioning of control.

The most important forward step would seem to be to insulate the advertiser from programming decisions. Some people will regard this idea as visionary—what we have, often comes to seem inevitable—but a closer look will show that the idea is entirely practical. Britain has developed a commercial television system which is supported by many of the same advertisers who support American television; the income of the British system, incidentally, has proved so unexpectedly large as almost to embarrass its leaders. The British system allows the advertiser to buy time for commercials but not to control programs.

* From Wednesday night schedule in Minneapolis.

The British law states:

> Nothing shall be included in any programmes broadcast by the Authority, whether in an advertisement or not, which states, suggests or implies, or could reasonably be taken to state, suggest or imply, that any part of any programme broadcast by the Authority which is not an advertisement has been supplied or suggested by an advertiser; and, except as an advertisement, nothing shall be included in any programme broadcast by the Authority which could reasonably be supposed to have been included therein in return for payment or other valuable consideration to the relevant programme contractor or Authority.

However, it is not necessary to cite the British system to make clear that what is being urged is practical. We can look at examples closer to home: our own newspapers and magazines. An advertiser does not expect to tell a magazine what story shall occupy the column adjoining his ad. He does not expect to tell a newspaper that his ad must adjoin a *pleasant* news story befitting his product image, with human interest and nothing controversial, and that he wants to review it for possible revisions before it is printed.

But we do not even have to go to the printed media for convincing evidence. We can turn to American television itself, or at least one corner of it: the area of news and public affairs. Here the system advocated is already in operation, and is proving itself over and over.

While much of television went into a spiral of conformity, television journalism continued to acquit itself with honor and often distinction. There is good reason for this. Newscasts, documentaries relating to current issues, and similar programs have been produced under a special set of circumstances. They are produced "under the supervision and control" of the network and are so announced. Here the network has assumed responsibility and exercised it. The advertiser, by definition and in fact, is out of the situation except as advertiser. He is, in this program area, not a censor and not an editor.

As we look back, we find that almost everything of importance that has happened in television has come about when this special set of circumstances existed.

As an example, take the remarkable Murrow-Friendly program *Clinton and the Law,* a CBS documentary about integration conflicts and pressures in one community—Clinton, Tennessee. Painstakingly and with enormous impact, the program presented the entire spectrum of opinion in the community. At one extreme this involved the filming of a meeting at which a much-publicized segregationist told his listeners, in the presence of the CBS cameras and microphones, that most current Supreme Court justices were Communists and that the presidential candidates being offered by the two major parties gave the electorate a choice between a rogue and a fool. Considered by the producers an essential part of the total spectrum, the sequence was included in the program. The program was sponsored by Pan-American Airways and produced "under the supervision and control of CBS News." Needless to say, the script was not submitted to Pan-American or to its advertising agencies for approval and revisions.

The imagination of any television writer can supply interesting dialogue for the script conference that, in this case, never happened. Would it be wise to give a nationwide platform to a man referring to the leading presidential candidates as "rogue" and "fool"? Would it not be best to take out the allegation that the Supreme Court justices were Communists? Would not some people believe he was speaking the truth? Or that the views expressed were those of Pan-American Airways? Would it not be safer to delete the whole sequence? In fact, would it not be better in the future to avoid problems of this sort by sticking to safer kinds of programming?

Clinton and the Law made a major contribution to the national thinking-through of a crucial problem. Prints of it are now in university and school film libraries in all parts of the United States. It is a permanent contribution to American historical archives. But it could only have been produced under the arrangement that applied in this case.

Then why not the same arrangement for other kinds of programs? The network has justified the distinction by saying that news concerns controversial ideas and issues. Does anyone imagine fiction-drama does not? Do the networks believe that

Ibsen, Strindberg, Shaw, O'Neill, Sherwood, and Kaufman did not deal with ideas and issues? As we have seen, the television dramatist strays into journalism as persistently as the television journalist strays into dramaturgy. No clear dividing lines separate the terms—which we must use because they are the best we have—like "news documentary," "factual film," "documentary drama," "drama," "fiction drama." When a writer turns to fiction rather than nonfiction, it is sometimes because he feels it will get him closer to truth. Both alike reflect the world and conflicting views about it. And if we want to prepare the soil, in television, for the growth of even one writer of stature, we shall have to accept the fact that fiction and drama deal with ideas as much as any newspaper front page. Any policy that treats news as significant but drama as a mere backdrop for a commercial is hanging out a sign that says, "Writer go home."

"Supervision and control" of the network does not mean, of course, that the network should produce all programs. It means only that the network should be responsible for balance, diversity, and quality—responsible to the public and to the Commission that represents it, not to the advertiser.

The network can perhaps exercise that responsibility best if it concentrates on newscasts and special events and enriches its schedule with the work of a diversity of independent producers, selected by it in exercise of its responsibility for diversity. And all this assumes, of course, that the ambiguous legal position of the network should be clarified and that it should be made responsible in law.

Who would lose by it? Not the networks; it would be their Magna Charta. Some network executives have tried to accomplish exactly what is here proposed. Sylvester Weaver, in the "magazine concept" which he advanced when he was president of the National Broadcasting Company, was moving in that direction. But apparently any network hesitates to put such a policy into effect by itself, lest its competitive position be undermined. The idea can probably be put into effect only by the authority or influence of government. Once in effect, almost everyone would gain by it and welcome it, including the advertiser.

In the United Kingdom the advertiser has quickly accepted this system. The advertiser accepts it in our own printed media. He accepts it in the sponsoring of news programs. The moment it is in effect at all networks simultaneously, he will accept it and even be thankful for it. For the first time he will be "off the hook" insofar as pressure groups are concerned. For the first time he will be able to participate in a vigorous and venturesome program service without being held responsible for every word uttered. No doubt he would, in time, bless the day when this system was put into effect, even though he may protest it now.

The advertiser placing a single commercial should be able to specify only its insertion within a block of time of uniform value, such as 8 to 11 P.M. An advertiser placing a *series* of commercials should know that within that same sort of block the commercials would be rotated automatically among all possible positions, so that an advertiser's message might one week follow a news program, another week a detective play, another week a documentary.

To the writer, a plan of this sort would open a new world. He would be able to deal with producers and editors who have authority and are not mere editorial errand boys. He would be able to work on program proposals with the knowledge that they would be considered in terms of their validity, not in terms of their applicability to a merchandising problem, not in relation to the attractions of coproduction deals.

The television writer knows that the potentialities of his medium have hardly been touched. The experiments of its early years have only hinted at what the future could hold. New worlds lie open to the coming dramatist; but he should also know that he may have to struggle for the right to explore those worlds. If he leaves it to others to shape the pattern of his profession, he may be doomed to the role of mouthpiece. If he wants something better he must speak for it. When he does, will be surprised at what he can achieve.

2. Techniques and Practices

2.   Techniques and Practices

THE previous pages have indicated the general nature of television as a writer's medium, as it has developed in somewhat over a decade. They also have sketched the professional problems that face the writer in television in the United States.

This section returns to the medium and documents comments made earlier. It also attempts to lay bare various technical matters by means of a guided tour through several dozen very brief script excerpts.

The art of moving, amusing, and informing audiences is not based on technical matters of the sort here discussed. Such technical knowledge is to the writer what paint chemistry is to the painter: necessary to the fulfillment of talent, no substitute for it. This is the craft part of the writer's task, the part that can readily be learned.

To the writer new to television, such matters are likely to loom unnecessarily large. Questions of practice and procedure leap to mind and seem to block even the beginning of work. In trying to clarify questions of this sort, we hope that talent will be helped to move more quickly to the real task at hand, whatever that may be. To save time and needless confusion is our one aim in this section.

Some of the excerpts presented on the following pages are from published scripts; the sources are indicated so that the reader can study these scripts further. Other excerpts are from unpublished production scripts. In a few cases the writer's name was not readily available or was in doubt. Our apologies for any omissions or errors that may have been made.

The page arrangement used for all excerpts is that which

is now most widely used. It is used by virtually all filmed series and has been adopted by some live series. It is the most readable of all forms and is also space-saving. The writer submitting a script to a series is advised to ascertain the page arrangement it uses.

1. TITLE PAGES

The main title page of a television script, as submitted by the writer, often contains no more than the title and the name of the author.

There may also be, in any corner, his address or the address of his agent. Some scripts are submitted in manuscript covers. An agent usually has a standard manuscript cover on which his name and address are printed. Manuscript covers are not essential, but they are certainly advisable in the case of long scripts.

A Walk Down the Hill, title page of one-hour script by Ernest Kinoy, originally telecast on CBS-TV.

A WALK DOWN THE HILL

by

Ernest Kinoy

2.   TITLE PAGES (*continued*)

If a script has been written for a particular series, the series title usually will be included.

Producers of some series ask the writer to include, on the title page or following page, a paragraph synopsizing the script. Some articles and books of advice to the television writer treat this as if it were a universal requirement, which it is not. It is a device useful on the formula series, where scripts usually are identical in emotional satisfaction and distinguishable largely by surface details. The capsule paragraph saves executive time. In the case of this *Lineup* script, an executive will be in a position to say, "We had a trophy room two weeks ago, we'd better hold this for at least a couple of months." Later the paragraph will also save time for a publicity writer and may eventually turn up in *TV Guide* and the newspaper boxes of recommended programs. Producers and writers dealing with material more dependent on character than on plot will find less value in these capsule paragraphs. Most anthology series have not had such a requirement. Most writers will want to resist it to the death.

"The Samuel McCutcheon Case," by Fred Eggers, for series *The Lineup.*

THE LINEUP

#157

"THE SAMUEL MCCUTCHEON CASE"

(A strangler loose in a city and
two victims who meet him, a big-game
hunter's final quarry, and a trophy
room becoming a morgue.)

by Fred Eggers
FIRST DRAFT

3.   TITLE PAGES (*continued*)

The main title page usually is followed by at least one additional title page, listing characters and sets. This page indicates the physical dimensions of the production and remains a convenient reference throughout work on the program.

On many filmed series, production is divided between scenes shot in a studio and scenes shot outdoors, on the studio lot or at other locations. A half-hour program may require one day of studio shooting, two of location shooting. Every part of such a schedule demands the earmarking and reserving of facilities, equipment, personnel. The process begins with the division between "interior" and "exterior" shooting, largely inherent in the script and tentatively indicated by the writer. The writer is thus at once involved in production economics.

Note that in the *Leave It to Beaver* script, the only exterior scene is already available on film, being used in identical form on each program. It is thus "stock" footage. Note also that the patio scene, though exterior in effect, will be shot in the studio. The patio is part of the standard studio set of the Cleaver home. Interior shooting may thus involve scenes not interior in effect.

The Beaver series is filmed but does not especially follow a cinematic tradition. It has strong unity of time and place, emphasis on character, little physical action. It could be produced live, on tape, or on film. Its production on film has distribution rather than production advantages. Pursuing quiet humor and unpretentious dramaturgy, some of its episodes may become television classics.

"Beaver's Accordion," by Joe Connolly and Robert Mosher, for series *Leave It to Beaver*. Gomalco Productions, Inc.

LEAVE IT TO BEAVER

"BEAVER'S ACCORDION"

CAST

JUNE
WARD
WALLY
BEAVER
EDDIE HASKELL
WHITEY
CLERK
MR. FRANKLIN

SETS

INTERIORS:

CLEAVER ENTRY HALL
    "   PATIO (ON STAGE)
    "   KITCHEN
    "   BOYS' ROOM
    "   LIVING ROOM
EXPRESS OFFICE
CLEAVER UPSTAIRS HALLWAY
    "   DEN

EXTERIORS:

CLEAVER FRONT DOOR (STOCK)

4.   TITLE PAGES (*continued*)

More representative of cinema tradition in its emphasis on mobility, visual variety, and outdoor action is this set list for a *Cheyenne* episode. This is a one-hour series.

Again some use is made of stock footage.

Since the set list occupies an entire page, the cast list in this case occupies an additional title page. A script for this series therefore has three title pages before the script itself.

"Bronco," teleplay by James O'Hanlon based on a novel by C. B. Kelland, for series *Cheyenne*. Warner Brothers Pictures, Inc.

SETS

EXTERIORS

    ADOBE HUT
    MAIN STREET, MIDWAY, TEXAS
    RICKY'S SHOP
    DRESSMAKER'S SHOP
    TENT
    SMALL RESTAURANT, MIDWAY
    BANK
    DIANA SALOON AND GAMBLING HALL
    DESERT ROAD
    MORAGA (STOCK)
        a) Street
        b) Saloon
        c) Warehouse
        d) Road
    DESERT
        a) Rocky area
        b) Hilltop overlooking desert
        c) Waterhole
        d) Sand dune

INTERIORS

    DIANA SALOON AND GAMBLING HALL
    BATHING ROOM AT DIANA SALOON
    DRESSMAKER'S SHOP
    RANCH HOUSE - a) Foyer; b) Living room;
                c) Study
    RICKY'S SHOP
    TENT
    RESTAURANT
    MARAGA SALOON AND WAREHOUSE

5.   TITLE PAGES (*continued*)

Some producers ask the writer to include in the cast list
brief character descriptions, as in this page from *Rawhide*.
Again, some articles and handbooks have mistakenly magnified
this into a universal requirement.

The supposed purpose is an aid to casting. The director who
does his own casting, as the best do, will hardly go by pigeon-
hole phrases. He goes by the image that forms in his mind as
he reads the script. The script may include a few descriptive
words as a character is introduced, but more important are
things said and done in response to the situations of the play.
The little phrases become serviceable mainly in large-scale
organizations, as a means for delegating work. They suggest
how such delegation is apt to lead to standardization. "We still
need two people," the casting assistant tells the talent representative on the phone. "One, a typical Easterner, eighteen years old;
and two, a distractingly beautiful girl of about thirty, a completely amoral opportunist." "I have exactly what you need,"
says the talent representative.

A mere listing of characters, without thumbnail description,
is sufficient on most anthology series, especially those dealing
in complex characters. Let the script define the characters.

On this page from *Rawhide,* a skillfully produced series, the
first four characters are not described, because they are fixtures
on the series.

"Incident on the Edge of Madness," by Herbert Little, Jr., and David
Victor, for series *Rawhide*.

CAST SHEET

GIL FAVOR........Eric Fleming

ROWDY YATES......Clint Eastwood

WISHBONE

PETE NOLAN.......Shep Wooley

JESSE CHILDRESS..He's about 30, an ignorant, hulking
                man, who just can't do anything right.
                Tenderness and violence vie for
                possession of him.

WARREN MILLETT...In his late 30's, sensitive Southern
                aristocrat, half crazed by the sting
                of defeat and the vision of a new
                Confederate Empire.

NARCIE..........About 30. A completely amoral oppor-
                tunist, distractingly beautiful in a
                dark, intense way. She'll fight,
                scratch, connive, seduce, do anything
                to share Millett's impossible fili-
                bustering scheme.

BOSTON..........18. A typical Easterner of the times,
                attracted to the West by the romance of
                the trail. Ingenuous, likeable on
                sight.

RAFE............A hard-bitten cowhand, leather-faced,
                trail-worn.

BRAD............Another trail hand, always horning for
                a scrape.

MAYOR HASLIP.....A middle-aged, ineffectual man. One of
                the Southerners eager only for peace
                and a chance to lick his wounds and re-
                store some kind of normalcy in the town
                of Niosha.

ZACHARIAH........An elderly Negro, completely disoriented
                by the course of events during the Civil
                War, Millett's retainer.

MUSHY...........Cook's louse.

6. OPENING

The television attitude toward openings is a heritage from radio rather than from theatre or film. Theatre and theatrical film can assume an audience that is seated, reasonably imprisoned, not likely to leave for some time except under extraordinary provocation. Television knows that its audience is uncommitted and unimprisoned, and that it has some choice. It has every temptation, if things are slow, to see what is doing on other channels. Every broadcast period begins with dial-wandering; the first job is to hold the wanderers.

In the early days of broadcast drama it seemed natural to begin with an announcement of matters to come, followed by a commercial, so that entertainment might then proceed with minimum interruption. Experience under increasingly competitive conditions revealed the risk: during the preliminaries the audience might go elsewhere. Hence increasing emphasis on immediate action, with explanations and commercial left to a later moment, a moment of heightened audience interest. The present excerpt, a portion of the teaser from *Tragedy in a Temporary Town,* was written to precede any mention of title, credits, or commercial.

Whereas theatrical tradition once favored expository openings involving minor characters, preparing an "entrance" for star performers, television more often introduces major conflicts and characters at once. Exposition is, at all costs, postponed.

Tragedy in a Temporary Town, by Reginald Rose; in A. S. Burack (ed.), *Television Plays for Writers.*

A lightly wooded section of ground...This area is at the edge of the trailer clearing. It is quite dark. We see several trees and bushes. Walking through them, toward the trailer camp, is Dotty Fisher. She is fifteen years old, not too attractive, quite high-strung yet slightly withdrawn. Her parents consider her a "nervous girl," and she does not relate especially well to her contemporaries or to her elders. She walks through the brush in the darkness for a moment, and then stops at a small tree. She begins to brush off her dress. Behind the tree we see another figure. We can only see that it is a boy or a man. No features are distinguishable. He is bent over tying up a small bundle of brushwood to take back for a laundry fire. He looks up at Dotty. She doesn't see him. He stands up, tiptoes over to her. Then he whispers, "Hey." She turns, startled, and he throws his arms about her, and tries to kiss her. She screams. He jumps back into the brush. She screams again louder, and now she starts toward the clearing screaming hysterically.

CUT TO:

The group of men at the tree. They are all on their feet, looking in the direction of the screams. The screams continue.

7.   OPENING (*continued*)

The sudden opening is by no means confined to the commercial series. Noncommercial programming is under equivalent pressures. Here a religious program uses an unconventional and effective means for rousing our curiosity on a matter of philosophy.

These are the opening moments.

"A Jewish Perspective," by Morton Wishengrad, for series *Directions '61*. Jewish Theological Seminary of America and ABC-TV.

FADE IN:

CU of narrator, head and shoulders.

> NARRATOR
> Once upon a time there was a Prince
> with an odd sense of humor. One day
> he seized an old scholar who was
> traveling on the King's Highway.

> SCHOLAR'S VOICE
> Don't kill me!

Pull back camera to show narrator holding the point of a
sword against the scholar's throat.

> NARRATOR
> If you want to live, tell me what
> Judaism means in exactly two words.

> SCHOLAR
> Two words!

> NARRATOR
> The whole meaning in two words!
> Neither more nor less.

> SCHOLAR
> All of Judaism in two words?

> NARRATOR
> Or else you die...

In an aside with a wink at the camera.

> This was a very mean Prince. Mind you,
> if he had said tell me what Judaism
> means in three words, even I could have
> answered. "Veahavta Lereach Kamocha."
> Thou shalt love thy neighbor as thyself.
> But two words. Impossible!

8.   OPENING (*continued*)

A television opening must, of course, not only round up an audience but the right sort of audience. A deceptive opening can boomerang.

This is an excerpt from an opening introducing a comedy. Its central character will die in the third act and the author wants us to accept this immediately and to have no maudlin feelings about it. The play has a fine comic climax in which a gravestone is hauled by moving company pulley to a point outside a sixth story tenement window so that the old man can see his gravestone. To establish the mood that will make such a climax both acceptable and delightful is clearly something of a challenge. The teaser for *The Explorer* accomplishes this with skill. It opens with a panning movement down a street of tenements. The excerpt continues from this point.

The Explorer, by Howard Rodman; in Florence Britton (ed.), *Best Television Plays, 1957*.

Suddenly, as we pass a tenement stoop, the door of the
building flies open and a 12-year-old boy, David, comes
leaping down the stairs. He turns left, runs two doors
up the street, careening off a passerby, and hurls himself into a store on the window of which is this legend:

> BARRABAS
> MONUMENTS AND STONE CUTTING
> PLAIN & FANCY

We follow David into the store, past some monuments plain
and fancy, past the wooden A-frame from which depends the
tackle to move the heavy granite blocks, and finally we
come with David to Barrabas himself, working diligently
on an inscription with hammer and chisel. The stone we
see is lettered, so far:

> Simon Feder
> 1884-195
> A
> good husband
> and a loving fa

Barrabas is at work on the "t" in "father" and he doesn't
stop or even look up when David enters.

> DAVID

Mr. Barrabas--

> BARRABAS
> David, tell your grandfather this is
> not cheese, it's stone. And it'll be
> done when it's done.

> DAVID
> Well, you better hurry up now, because
> they just sent me for the doctor, and
> it's going to be a shame if grandpa
> doesn't get to see it. I just thought
> I'd let you know!

Out of the store goes David. Now Barrabas looks up,
straightening his back, then to work again with a sense
of increased urgency.

9.   OPENING (*continued*)

In general, a narrative opening is considered risky. A man at a desk is considered a suicidal opening. If, as illustrated here, a high-budget sponsored program did risk such an opening, there must have been special circumstances to justify it. The special circumstances were these: The narrator at the table was an important actor, Claude Rains; the broadcast was based on a best-selling book, *A Night to Remember;* and the telecast had been highly publicized. Also, the writers were laying the foundation for an unusual and powerful sequence that required this sort of preparation.

The teaser sequence was in two portions. The first consisted of narration by a visible narrator, while the second used a different kind of narrative technique. It seems worth while to illustrate the contrast of the two techniques and the effectiveness of their combined use in *A Night to Remember.*

The present excerpt illustrates the first portion; the succeeding excerpt, the second portion.

A Night to Remember, adapted by George Roy Hill and John Whedon from the book by Walter Lord; in *Prize Plays of Television and Radio 1956.*

FADE UP narrator seated at table.

                    NARRATOR
          In 1898 a struggling author named Morgan
          Robertson wrote this book.

He picks up the book.

          It was fiction. It looked into the future
          and told the story of a fabulous Atlantic
          liner, far larger than any that had ever
          been built. Its displacement was 70,000
          tons, its length 800 feet, its top speed
          25 knots. On a day in April she departed
          on a voyage across the North Atlantic.
          Her capacity was 3,000 people, but since
          she was considered unsinkable, she carried
          lifeboats for only a fraction of that
          number. Four days later on a cold April
          night, she raced across the North Atlantic,
          heedless of iceberg warnings, struck an
          iceberg and went down, carrying the rich
          and complacent aboard her to the bottom.
          It symbolized the end of an age, of luxury,
          class inequality, of supreme self-confidence
          of man against fate. Robertson named his
          book Futility. The name he gave his ship
          was the Titan. In 1912, fourteen years
          after this book was published, a British
          shipping company, the White Star Line,
          built a fabulous Atlantic liner, far larger
          than any that had ever been built.

CUT TO film shot of whistle blasting.

          SOUND: WHISTLE, DEEP BLAST

DISSOLVE TO the bridge. CAPTAIN SMITH in command. WILDE
and another officer.

                    CAPTAIN
          Cast off spring lines.

10.   OPENING (*continued*)

Now the patience of the opening begins to prove its value, as the story of the fictional *Titan* is paralleled, point by point, by the story of the historic *Titanic*. At the same time, our drama too is beginning. As the narrator makes his points, now unseen, the departure of the *Titanic* is dramatized by means of a selection of stimulating details, sweeping camera movements, dialogue vignettes, sound effects, music. The script here asks for utmost virtuosity in studio production. Meanwhile, the narration continues.

For the writer new to television, it is not easy to appreciate the amount of action that can, as in this excerpt, accompany a narration without interfering with its rhythm and meaning.

Part of the power of this opening is in the total attention it enlists. This is developed step by step from the quiet, risky beginning.

Program title and opening credits follow completion of the parallel details. The entire teaser takes several minutes.

A Night to Remember.

                              OFFICER
                        (through megaphone)
                    Cast off bow lines!

                              NARRATOR
                    Her displacement was 66,000 tons, her
                    length 882 feet, her top speed 25 knots.

                              OFFICER
                    Lines cast off, sir.

                              CAPTAIN
                    Quarter speed astern.

                              WILDE
                    Quarter speed astern.

CUT TO hand moving telegraph.

          SOUND: TELEGRAPH

CUT TO film shot of whistle.

          SOUND: DEEP WHISTLE BLAST.

CUT TO deck, lower level.

          SOUND: CROWD NOISES - SHOUTING GOODBYE -
          BAND PLAYING IN BACKGROUND - TUG WHISTLES

People leaning over rail, waving. Dolly past them slowly.
They are covered with confetti, cheering, shouting mes-
sages.

                              NARRATOR
                    On April 10th, 1912, she departed
                    Southampton on her maiden voyage to
                    New York.

The camera starts to boom to upper deck between life-
boats. People above also waving.

                    Her capacity was 3,000 people, but since
                    she was considered unsinkable, she carried
                    lifeboats for only a fraction of that number.

11. CREDIT SEQUENCE

In the theatrical film, in past decades, artists and technicians were usually credited at the beginning, along with the main title. In television the tendency has been to relegate a large portion of the credits to the end of the program. Only the most essential are included with the opening title.

Occasionally, this opening title and a few credits of special value are handled so that they do not interrupt the story launched in the teaser, but are briefly superimposed over it.

In *Tragedy in a Temporary Town*, Reginald Rose has planned the teaser, the title and credit sequence, and the following scene for continuing action, without letup of tension.

A portion of the teaser has already been quoted. Here is the title and credit sequence.

Tragedy in a Temporary Town.

CUT TO the group of men at tree. They are on their
feet, looking in the direction of the screams. Screams
continue.

CUT TO big close-up of the water pipe. Pike's bucket is
full to overflowing. The water continues to run into it.

SUPERIMPOSE titles and credits.

While credits are running we stay on bucket. We hear but
do not see the following. The screams become louder and
louder.

                    PIKE
          What the heck is that?

                    SANKEY
          Hey, look at her!

                    ANDERSON
          It's the Fisher kid.

The screams, at top peak now, degenerate into loud sobs
as Dotty reaches the group. We still hold on bucket
overflowing.

                    BEGGS
          Hey, take it easy.

                    ANDERSON
          What's a matter? Ya hurt or something?

                    DORAN
          She don't look hurt.

                    BEGGS
          We oughta make her sit down.

                    PIKE
          Listen, what happened to you?

                    BEGGS
          She's hysterical. Hey, stop it now.
          Cut it out.

Credits are finished. We CUT TO the group of men
surrounding the still sobbing girl...

12.   CREDIT SEQUENCE (*continued*)

In informational as well as other kinds of programs, the on-the-wing treatment of opening credits has become common. This excerpt is from an arresting, penetrating series of television essays by Albert Burke, a former supervisor of graduate studies at Yale University. This "essay" deals with Cuba and has opened with footage of the Castro revolution. Now it is showing the Cuba known to tourists before the Castro uprising. Burke, for the moment, is an off-screen ("O. S.") voice.

"Cuba: The Battle of America," in the series *A Way of Thinking,* written and narrated by Dr. Albert Burke. Metropolitan Broadcasting Company.

Footage of "tourist alley" - casinos, exotic restaurants, etc.

                    BURKE (O. S.)
To most American tourists to Cuba, this
is Cuba...It isn't Cuba at all, of course.
It is a transplanted bit of the United
States from the airconditioned hotels to
the table linen and silver serving dishes
in the restaurants. Most of what you see
on the screen was built by Americans, in
fact. In Havana's case, much of that
transplanted bit of North America was
built by a very special group of Americans
who have given to many Cuban people a very
peculiar picture of what life in America
must be like...

                                        CUT TO:

Albert Burke, standing in spotlight.

                    BURKE
John Q. there had a whale of a time in
Havana back in 1958, several weeks before
Castro reached that city. I am Albert
Burke. I will try to tell you why that
was the case.

13. CREDIT SEQUENCE (*continued*)

Titles and credits have been the subject of considerable inventiveness, in the effort to make them a positive rather than negative element in program openings. The first few moments of *Super Circus* are an example, using the fluidity of television to create an opening that is completely in the circus spirit.

Super Circus, ABC-TV.

MUSIC: CIRCUS BAND

Screen is filled by two words painted on tightly
stretched paper:

S U P E R

C I R C U S

Clown's head crashes through the paper from behind,
laughing.

Picture starts to SPIN, electronically.

DISSOLVE TO:

CU: spinning baton of girl juggler. PULL BACK to
full shot of girl.

14. SETTING

In launching his story, fiction or nonfiction, the writer soon has the problem of defining the setting of his action. When the curtain rises in a theatre, the audience usually sees an entire set. Attention may then be directed to particular details. The progression is almost necessarily from the whole to the part. Film and television can reverse this procedure; they can begin with the smallest detail, then pull back to show the over-all setting in which it exists.

In this excerpt, the setting is the board room of the magazine *Event,* "outranked only by *Life* and *Look*." The board room looks like other board rooms, and the writer therefore does not begin with the whole room, but with a close-up of a copy of the magazine. As we pull back, we find that it is lying on a board room table, which is surrounded by executives. The close-up beginning has told us more about the men in the room, and the business they are engaged in, than any larger view would have done.

Television is especially inclined toward this procedure, because in any over-all view details may be lost in the mosaic texture of the screen. On the other hand, the detail alone can fill the screen with clarity. The audience often remembers a setting by the small detail that introduced it. The detail *becomes* the set. A room is "the room of the old alarm clock"; another, "the room with the cobweb."

Paper Foxhole, by James Elward; in *Prize Plays of Television and Radio, 1956.*

FADE IN:

A tight shot of the cover of a copy of Event Magazine,
a publication outranked only by Life and Look. The
camera pulls back to show the table it rests on and
the men seated around this small paneled conference
room. Four men sit around the table: ANDREW J.
FOGARTY, the publisher of Event, and three of his
editorial staff. Fogarty is a portly man in his
fifties; the others are younger but only a shade less
pompous. They are MACAULEY (Editor of National Affairs,
according to the sign by his place), SANDERS (Editor
of European Affairs), and FERGUSON (Editor of Baltic
affairs). One place remains vacant at the table:
the Editor of Far Eastern Affairs. A pretty young
stenographer is seated away from the table, ready to
take notes. It is obvious that Fogarty and his staff
are waiting with no great patience for the last, late
member of the conference. Fogarty checks his watch
and then the clock on the wall behind him. The time
is 12:03. Over the clock hangs the magazine motto:
"Each moment is an Event."

15.   SETTING (*continued*)

If television has special interest in the outward progression, from the detail to the whole, it also makes frequent use of the opposite, more familiar progression. In outdoor drama it has every reason to do so, to take advantage of the excitement of a spacious long shot. In this *Rawhide* sequence, it is not details but light and shadow, form and movement that make the picture. We see the cattle drive first in the distance, in a setting of vast space. The next shot brings it closer. The third shot brings us to the central figure, trail boss Gil Favor.

Rawhide.

FADE IN:

1 EXT. DRIVE LONG SHOT (DAY)

In the distance, rising cloud of dust hovers over
the seemingly endless column of cattle. The herd is
moving right to left, making a curve as it approaches
CAMERA. Behind the cattle, the vast range and stony
grandeur of the terrain stand out. The BAWLING of
the cattle is HEARD along with the YELLING of riders.

2 EXT. DRIVE MED. SHOT - HERD ON THE MOVE (DAY)

The herd surges toward CAMERA. HOOFS BEAT loudly on
the caked surface of the prairie. SHOUTING of riders
cracks over the almost unbearably loud HOLLERING of
the herd. Dust swirls.

3 EXT. DRIVE MOVING SHOT - GIL FAVOR (DAY)

He maneuvers his horse behind the point riders. His
eyes rove with concern over the moving herd. During
the following, SHOTS of the herd, ROWDY, PETE and the
riders are seen. The YELLING of the cowboys punctuates
Gil's words.

16.   SETTING (*continued*)

When a play is produced live or on tape, the writer is usually limited to the amount of scenery that can be built in a gymnasium-sized studio. This may include a number of sets, if they are not especially large. When only one major set is used, it may be a set consisting of many parts.

In the business office set used in *Patterns,* action flows from Mr. Staples' private office, to the outer office of his secretary, to the corridor, to the conference room. In this brief excerpt we move through virtually the entire set, as the camera follows the action. In an earlier television period it was common for the camera to explore the setting at the opening of the play, for no apparent reason except to acquaint the audience with the *mise en scène*. This was generally undramatic and had the added disadvantage of making the audience conscious of mechanics. In the present excerpt we have a completely "motivated" camera movement. We are seeing the set only in the course of pursuing the characters. The sequence starts in Mr. Staples' inner office. He is the new executive, and Marge is to be his secretary. Upset over the personnel shake-up, she has been crying.

A special value of the multiple-part set will become clear later. Once the set has been established, the writer can jump at any time from one part of it to another, and in so doing make jumps in time as well as in space. He thus has a good deal of flexibility in the use of time.

Patterns, in *Patterns: Four Television Plays,* by Rod Serling.

                              MARGE
            You're inheriting his title, Mr. Staples,
            but it's a package deal. You'll get his
            heartache, too.

She walks out of the office, Fred staring after her.
Andy comes out of his office, sees Marge quickly dabbing
at her eyes. He turns to Fred, who comes out of his
office.

                              ANDY
            Ready, Fred? It's about that time.

                              FRED
            Yeah. Yeah, I'm all set.

                              ANDY
            Good.

They start up the corridor toward the conference room.
Andy, as usual, pauses by the water cooler.

                              FRED
            Andy...

                              GORDON
                        (passing them)
            You gentlemen ready?

                              FRED
            We'll be right in...I never wanted to knife
            you, Andy. I never wanted to --

                              ANDY
            I'm braced now. Don't make it any harder.
            The last ten years - all pointing to this
            next minute - and I'm braced for it now.
            So for God's sake, Fred, let's not have any
            unburdening now.

He walks on ahead and into the conference room.

17.   SETTING (*continued*)

In this live-television excerpt we begin with a man standing in *no setting*. He is in a spotlight surrounded by darkness—in other words, *in limbo*.

Although the narrator appears in limbo, each scene has scenery. This is at first observed at a distance, also surrounded by darkness; we then move toward it and, from this point, follow a naturalistic style within each individual scene. At the end of the scene the camera reverses the procedure, pulling back from the scene and ending on the narrator, again surrounded by darkness. This technique, in which each scene comes to us out of darkness, seems appropriate to a play in which the narrator is giving us recollections from a dim past.

This method is merely one of innumerable ways in which narrators can be used. It is illustrated here because the narrator *in limbo* is almost unknown in theatrical film.

Parenthetically, the excerpt also illustrates the latitude available to the writer in the choice of conventions. In this excerpt the narrator talks about the past from the vantage point of the present, as most narrators do. But at the instant the scene lights up in the background, he switches to the present tense and seems to live in the period of the story: "That's Jeff, my father. He's a shingler." The procedure is not usual but completely acceptable; the lighting up of the scene is, for us too, the moment of transition into living in the past. The writer sticks to the procedure in later transitions.

A Matter of Pride, adapted by Frank D. Gilroy from the short story "The Blue Serge Suit," by John Langdon; in *Best Television Plays, 1957.*

Fade in on the narrator, a man in his forties, standing alone.

                    NARRATOR
          There are times when all at once you stop
          being a kid...When it happens, you know.
          It happened to me when I was sixteen. I
          was living with my father then.

Behind the narrator lights come up on a kitchen where
Jeff, 38, is very solicitously whetting the blade of a
hatchet.

          That's Jeff, my father. He's a shingler.
          He's in a good frame of mind because he
          starts a new job this morning. It's the
          first one he's had in two months. On
          the last job he got in a fight with the
          superintendent. He won the fight but he
          lost the job. That happened to him a lot.
          It got so that nobody wanted to hire him
          even though he was one of the best shinglers
          in the business.

Jeff goes to the doorway and calls.

                    JEFF
          You almost ready for breakfast, Neal?

We don't hear Neal's reply.

          Well, come on then. I've got a surprise.

Jeff resumes whetting the hatchet. Now Neal, 16, enters.

                    NARRATOR
          That's me. I look confused because my
          father hasn't touched that hatched in two
          months. It could mean only one thing.

We go past the narrator into the scene proper.

                    NEAL
          You got a job?

18.   SETTING (*continued*)

In the previous excerpt the narrator was in limbo, the scenes had scenery. Here the arrangement is reversed. The dramatic vignettes are in limbo while the narrator has a setting. At least, he is first introduced in a setting; later parts of his narration are off screen.

The *Omnibus* series has specialized in celebrities as narrators (see pp. 10–11). This script, dramatizing the growth of the presidency and telecast on election eve, was narrated by Mc-George Bundy, a Harvard University dean, later close adviser to President Kennedy.

At various points in this program historic conflicts were established by presenting statesmen in brief vignettes in limbo. Sometimes they merely stood in spotlights, arranged in a geographical pattern. Giving somewhat the feeling of figures on an international chessboard, the technique was appropriate to the content.

If dramatic vignettes can be in limbo and narrators can be in limbo, can scenery be eliminated entirely? One of the most memorable television achievements was a serialized *Crime and Punishment* telecast by WCBS-TV, New York. Chairs and tables were used, but no walls. Scenes were played in strong spotlights, without intrusion of irrelevant detail. The effect was powerful. The earlier *Cameo Playhouse* used the same technique. Innumerable circumstances conspire to discourage its growth. Sponsors fear the impression will be that of a shoestring operation. And union contracts demand minimum crews whether needed or not, thus tending to make superfluous realism a vested interest.

"He Shall Have Power," by James Lee, for series *Omnibus*. Robert Saudek Associates.

> NARRATOR
> England's Lloyd George was humorously
> cavalier about the impossible task they
> faced.

Lloyd George in a spotlight.

> LLOYD GEORGE
> Please refresh my memory. Is it Upper
> Silesia or Lower Silesia we are giving
> away?

> NARRATOR (O.S.)
> Clemenceau was Gallic.

Pan has brought us to Clemenceau in another spotlight.

> CLEMENCEAU
> God gave us the Ten Commandments and we
> broke them. Wilson has given his fourteen
> points...We shall see.

> NARRATOR (O.S.)
> The world watched the bargaining table.
> Bolshevik Russia was less than a year
> old, but its leader, Lenin, the Father
> of the Revolution, ventured an opinion
> that might come from Moscow today.

Lenin, in another spotlight, is brought into the frame.

> LENIN
> The aggressive imperialism of these
> groups has unmasked itself. On the one
> side there will be the bourgeois system
> engaged in a strife between two coalitions
> of confessed plunderers, and on the other
> side a Socialist Soviet Republic living
> in peace.

19.   CAMERA USAGE

Various excerpts have suggested that the writer is at times
concerned with camera directions, whether in filmed, taped, or
live television. Television film production expects more of the
writer in this respect than does live television, as we shall see in
several examples.

Every camera shot involves decisions on what to include and
what to exclude. The writer's camera directions are sometimes
concerned with this function of excluding. The present excerpt
is an example.

The Bob Cummings Show, by Paul Hennig and Phil Shuken, in Irving
Settel (ed.), *Best Television Humor.*

1. OFFICE - DAY

   Open on a close-up of Schultzy seated at her desk
   looking up with a hurt, rapturous expression on her
   face. Over this close-up we hear Bob's voice. He
   is speaking softly and romantically.

                         BOB (O.S.)
           Darling, listen to me...I know you've seen
           me going out with other girls...lots of them
           ...beautiful girls...but they meant nothing
           to me. Don't you know that?

   Schultzy pouts and shakes her head "No."

           It's always been you. Won't you let me
           prove it?

   Schultzy hesitates as if fighting.

           Tonight? Please?

   Schultzy gives in, nods assent.

           Oh thank you, darling! I'm looking forward
           to our first date.

   The camera pulls back to reveal that Bob is standing
   in front of the desk facing the studio and talking
   on the phone. Schultzy has merely been observing
   and living vicariously.

           I'll pick you up on the corner across
           from the Girls' Club at seven-thirty.
           Bye Dorothy.

20.   CAMERA USAGE (*continued*)

On the *Shari Lewis Show* the camera is not a mere eavesdropper. It is addressed as a person—not a collection of people, but an individual. Thus, it is appropriate that Shari "motions the camera to come in closer" for confidential information. Camera motion is here planned to heighten a feeling of identification with the events on the program, to make the young viewer feel a participant.

"Christmas Show," by Saul Turteltaub, for *Shari Lewis Show*. Tarcher Productions in association with NBC-TV.

FADE IN:

Standard Opening.

                                        FADE OUT

FADE IN:

CU Shari in front of Christmas tree. Interior. Shari
is hanging decorations on tree, putting on tinsel, and
she has box in front of her from which she is taking
decorations.

                    SHARI
              (looks around, motions camera
              to come in closer)
        If I tell you a secret, can you keep it?
        Where will you keep it??   Some place
        no one can find it O.K.???   Well, I'm
        decorating this tree for a surprise
        Christmas party...Yep...Really, and you
        know who the surprise is for?
              (starts taking out long row
              of letters)
        Yep, you guessed it...
              (holds letters apart; they say
              "Mr. Goodfellow")
        Right...Mr. Goodfellow.

21.   CAMERA USAGE (*continued*)

In this excerpt it is the need for special emphasis that motivates a camera direction.

Kathy, the little girl in the *Father Knows Best* family, has been playing persistently with an imaginary companion called Oscar. The parents, Jim and Margaret, have begun to worry about her obsession with this fantasy and have tried vainly to cajole her into other interests. Finally they try an opposite tack; they pretend they, too, see Oscar. They are now entering the dinette for supper.

"Kathy Wins an Oscar," by Earle Doud and Robert Foshko, for series *Father Knows Best*.

                         JIM
          Oscar...Kathy...after you. Kathy,
          your regular chair.

Kathy sits hesitantly, watching the goings-on. Jim now
conducts "Oscar" to the seat opposite, pulling the chair
back and easing "Oscar" into the table for his comfort.

                         JIM
          And Oscar, right here. If you will...
          Is that a little too close? Sorry.
          There, how's that? Fine.

Jim sits in the third chair, between them.

                         JIM
          Now tell me, Oscar, how are you getting
          along in school?...Is that so? I admire
          someone who takes school seriously and
          studies hard. Don't you, Kathy?

Katherine is staring at the empty chair.

CLOSE SHOT OF CHAIR

Empty.

FULL SHOT

                         KATHY
          I don't feel so good.

22. CAMERA USAGE (*continued*)

In the film field the traditional unit of production is the shot. Each shot is "set up," lighted, rehearsed and photographed separately. In theatrical-film production hours may be spent on a single ten-second shot. Television economics requires a faster production pace and encourages a less drastic fragmentation into shots, but is still usually planned in terms of shots. There are exceptions, in which programs or major sequences are photographed as a unit, sometimes by several cameras in the live-television manner. Comedy programs performed before audiences would belong in this category.

If a program is to be produced in the normal manner, the tele-film writer writes his script in shots, and he numbers the shots. This excerpt includes a scene in a dressmaker's shop, which the writer has written in two shots. In the first (Number 18) the camera is to be aimed toward the door; the second (Number 19) will use the opposite angle. The director may modify the plan. He may decide to carry the action in the first shot further, duplicating part of the second, so as to include the girl's "stunned paralysis." This will enable the editor to cut back to this angle in the middle of shot Number 19. But though it is understood that the director may decide to provide such alternatives, the writer is still expected to specify a succession of shots that will provide a practical and efficient minimum.

This *Cheyenne* one-hour television episode included 172 shots. Frequently used abbreviations: BG for background, FG for foreground.

"Bronco."

>   McNALLY
>   (chuckles)
>   Why, you're one of the family! - will
>   be soon, anyhow.

Bronco smiles almost shyly.

>   BRONCO
>   Hope the rest of the family still feels
>   that way about it, sir.

>   McNALLY
>   (indicating shop)
>   She's right in there, son. Why don't
>   you go ask her?

Answering the old man's wink with a grin, Bronco
goes into:

18 INT. DRESSMAKER'S SHOP. ENTRANCE IN BG

In fg, attended by DRESSMAKER, Redemption is
struggling into button-up-back dress. ENTERING in
bg, Bronco approaches. Dressmaker sees him, is
about to protest, but he motions her to silence and
away from Redemption, steps into her place and takes
over the buttoning.

19 REVERSE. REDEMPTION AND BRONCO

Bronco, buttoning girl from behind, pauses and very
deliberately plants a lingering kiss on her bare
shoulder. She endures the kiss in stunned paralysis;
then, breaking it, whirls upon him with a protest on
her lips, does a second big take, and screaming
joyously:

>   REDEMPTION
>   Bronco!

throws herself into his embrace and they kiss
fervently.

23. CAMERA USAGE (*continued*)

Though the live-television writer may provide camera directions for any of various reasons mentioned and to be mentioned, he is not expected to plan each scene in terms of shots. The fact that this excerpt includes no shot breakdown does not mean it is to be photographed in one shot. More likely a half dozen will be used. Any important scene may be covered by two, three, or four different cameras; the director will cut from one to another, using shots of various kinds. The placement and use of the cameras necessarily depend on set design; set and camera usage must be planned together, and planned in relation to the placement and movement of the actors. In this scene there is also the problem that while Willie does the talking, the reactions of Gerta and Borden, to him and to each other, are more important. For all these reasons, the writer for live television leaves it to the director to work out the shots. The writer specifies what the actors will say and do; within the individual scene, these are his main functions. The setting of this excerpt is a cafeteria, where Horace Mann Borden, once a world-renowned boy prodigy who at the age of twelve had discussed Einstein's theories before the combined physics faculties of Harvard and M.I.T., now works as a waiter.

Man on the Mountaintop, by Robert Alan Aurthur, in Gore Vidal (ed.), *Best Television Plays.*

                         WILLIE
That's a very good prodigy. Gerta, if ever
you wanted to know what a prodigy looked
like, this is one. You see what happens
when you have brains and think too much.
You work in a crummy cafeteria. Prodigy,
say hello to your neighbor.

                         GERTA
                  (very embarrassed)
Willie, please!

                         WILLIE
Now I'll tell you what I'm going to do.
Fifty cents if you give me the answer to
the following question. You ready?

                         GERTA
Please, Willie, don't.

                         WILLIE
This is how he makes his movie money, Gerta,
wait'll you see. This prodigy goes to three
movies a day. You ready, Horace Mann?

Gerta starts to get up, but Willie pulls her down again.

How much, within three seconds you tell me,
how much is five hundred and seventy-eight
times three hundred and nine?

                         BORDEN
One hundred and seventy-eight thousand six
hundred and two.

                         WILLIE
Let me check that...Right, absolutely right.

He takes a coin from his pocket and flips it into the
air. Borden lets the coin fall on the floor.

24.   DIALOGUE PERSPECTIVE

In the theatre our attention usually goes to the person speaking; our eyes tend to follow dialogue like a ping-pong game. Only unexpected action distracts attention from speaker to listener. Film and television have more rigid control over audience attention. The writer may want to specify camera usage that will direct attention to a nonspeaker.

In *Tragedy in a Temporary Town* a group of men have crowded into one of the trailers and are feverishly planning to "do something" about the "attack" on a girl of the camp. Beggs, who is disturbed by the vigilante spirit, leaves the trailer. The writer asks that we continue to hear the men in the trailer, so that the threat of their plans continues to mount, but that the camera follow Beggs. Nothing could more effectively induce us to identify ourselves with Beggs and the feelings of dissent forming in him. To have him verbalize his feelings at this point would strike a false note; the point of his plight is his aloneness. Here the essence of the situation is dramatized by a simple device: detachment of the all-important visual spotlight from the sound source.

The dramatic implications of this device have concerned film makers since the first days of the sound film, and are still being explored. Directors and editors may, for example, decide on "reaction shots" for many reasons. But the writer should also think of the basic device as a writing tool, that can sometimes speak more meaningfully than words.

Tragedy in a Temporary Town.

                              DORAN
                    ...We're transients, man! That's like
                    garbage. There's nobody watching out for
                    us. We gotta protect our own! Now stop
                    giving me a hard time, and get back to
                    your trailer. We're comin' around to get
                    your list.

Beggs stares at Doran, and Doran stares back hard. Then
finally Beggs walks out of the trailer, shouldering the
men aside. As he walks out, we hear Doran continue.

CUT TO:

Outside of trailer.

                          DORAN (Off)
                    Now who's with me in this thing?

We hear a lusty chorus of assents. Beggs turns and
looks somberly at the trailer.

                    Okay. Now...Repulski, Harris, Muller,
                    Sankey, are the guards. Make a ring
                    around this place. Nobody goes in or
                    out, right? I mean if you have to bust
                    somebody, so bust 'em.

There is an answering mumble.

                    Okay, get goin'.

The guards come filing out of the trailer. Beggs
watches them. They disperse.

25. DIALOGUE PERSPECTIVE (*continued*)

The writer may want to put the visual spotlight elsewhere than on the sound source for a number of reasons. This excerpt illustrates a simple and practical reason: necessary identifications.

Parenthetically, the excerpt illustrates the standard procedure by which the telefilm writer defines each shot, going from the larger to the smaller categories. First designating the shot as interior (INT) or exterior (EXT), he then identifies the place, the time of day, the kind of camera shot, and the content of the shot. Common abbreviation: MED FULL for medium full.

"Death Takes an Encore," by Frank Kane, for *Mickey Spillane Series.* Revue Productions, Inc.

FADE IN:

1   INT. CORRIDOR OUTSIDE MIKE HAMMER'S OFFICE.
    CAMERA HOLDS on frosted glass bearing the legend:
    "Mike Hammer, Private Investigator. Entrance Room
    812."

                    TERRELL
              (Shrill voice, thru door)
         I killed him, I tell you. I killed
         him.

                                        DISSOLVE TO:

2   INT. MIKE HAMMER'S OFFICE. DAY. MED FULL.
    Mike Hammer is sitting behind his desk, fingering a
    clipping. In the customer's chair is Abel Terrell,
    an old man showing signs of a terrific mental strain.
    His clothes hang baggily, as though he had lost a
    lot of weight. There is a stubble along his chin
    line. He is shaking.

                    TERRELL
         Can't you understand? I killed him.

                    MIKE
         Calm down. Let's take it from the
         top. You killed him. Why?

                    TERRELL
         He would have ruined me. I had to
         kill him.

                    MIKE
         When was this?

26. DIALOGUE PERSPECTIVE (*continued*)

Still another reason is illustrated in this passage by a documentary writer of the British Broadcasting Corporation. The camera has introduced us to a group of leading citizens in a South African community, discussing apartheid. Toward the end of the sequence we continue to hear their voices, while the visual spotlight introduces new material. This makes an ironic commentary on the talk heard. In a sense, picture and sound are contesting each other.

For "dissolve," the British use the term "mix." Credits also follow a wording not used in the United States, where the form of credits has become standardized by union agreement (pp. 163–165).

The Wind of Change, devised by Denis Mitchell. British Broadcasting Corporation.

MANAGER OF LARGE STORE
South Africa is disliked in the outside
world. They don't see the other picture...
the lovely picture.

EDITOR
So that Africa is being disliked because
the Press, the Opposition Press, dislikes
us. All reports that go from South Africa
are sent over by the Opposition Press.

MANAGER OF LARGE STORE
Well, my experience is this. I have been
through the Scandinavian islands...and I
feel that the women there work as hard as
our natives. They get about the same wages,
salary, as the natives in this country.

MIX:

Newspaper headlines:

1. "Multiracial Sport Banned at Varsity"
2. "Court Told Mafeking Gaoler Forced Women to Strip"
3. "Man Seen with Black Girl Shot in Escape"

ANOTHER MAN IN THE SAME GROUP
(meanwhile, off)
I want to tell you that in this country
we are worrying too much about the native
question. I think they are enjoying more
privileges than many other people in the
rest of the world. We are treating them
very well, up to their standards.

27. DIALOGUE AND ACTION

Several of our excerpts pose problems about the relationship of words and actions. Clearly, even simple actions can compel our attention more rapidly and surely than words. At the same time, a few words can alter and even reverse the meaning of an action and its impact on us. The language of action has a fundamental appeal that antedates words. Words are a late historic arrival and do their work slowly and uncertainly. For many meanings we depend on words, but dare not depend on them too heavily lest we lose contact with our more fundamental natures.

Some of the implications for the writer are pursued in the next few excerpts. In the first of these, spoken words are suppressed. The events portrayed would surely involve dialogue, but the writer has decided not to use it. What has he gained?

One gain is in rhythm. Speech would impose on the sequence its own natural timing. With the advent of sound, this factor virtually wiped out a long tradition of film comedy. A sequence of this sort illustrates the intermittent effort to recapture the lost values. The writer is shaking off the shackles of speech to create a stylized effect, which in this case has comic value. The convention here adopted is readily accepted by audiences, and it is perhaps too seldom used. The sequence would be accompanied by music, and this would heighten the stylized effect.

Paper Foxhole.

DISSOLVE TO:

Film shot of Washington, D.C., view from the air. The
shot includes the Pentagon.

CUT TO:

A close shot of an officer's shoulder. The wearer is a
brigadier general (one star). The camera pulls back and
we see he is seated at a desk which carries the sign:
General Phipps, Far Eastern Affairs. Phipps is a thin,
middle-aged man who looks far too shy to be a general.
He appears faintly puzzled by the report which he is now
reading, but when he finishes it, he sighs, and taking
the report with him, rises.

CUT TO:

Tight shot of second military shoulder. This is a major
general (two stars). The camera pulls back. The sign
on this desk says: General Ames, Far Eastern Affairs.
Island Bases. Phipps stands behind Ames, who is much
more assured-looking than he, and watches him finish the
still-growing report. When Ames does, he looks at
Phipps, with the gravity of the situation. Without a
word, they pick up the report which is still growing,
and move quickly off camera.

CUT TO:

Tight shot of third military shoulder. This belongs to
a lieutenant general (three stars). The camera pulls
back. The sign on this desk is: General March, Pacific
Island Bases, Task Strategy. The report General March
(a florid man in his fifties) is reading is even thicker,
and he reads it with growing astonishment. Phipps and
Ames stand behind him, watching him nervously. When
March finishes the last page he looks at the other two.
He rises silently. All three faces are incredibly grim.

28.   DIALOGUE AND ACTION (*continued*)

Here again, spoken words are suppressed, but not for comic reasons. Again, rhythm is involved. The original communication between interviewer and interviewees—Indians living in South Africa—was presumably laborious. It may have involved interpreters. Use of the original sound would presumably stretch the sequence beyond its value and sacrifice any sense of organization. By distilling from his interviews the headshakes and accompanying them with abbreviated questions paralleling each other in form, the producer-writer has achieved something that is organized like a chart, while retaining the humanity and impact of the filmed material. Again stylization is achieved.

The technique might, under some circumstances, raise a question of authenticity. Obviously we must take it on faith that the headshakes were responses to the questions posed in the final sound track. One answer to this is that there are so many ways of deceiving an audience via film or tape that a journalist or documentarian must necessarily be accepted by an audience on faith—or else be rejected. There is no better argument for a clear allocation of editorial responsibility in television.

The Wind of Change.

Shots of the Indian quarter of Potgietersrust:

1. An Indian.

                          NARRATOR (O.S.)
                    Have you got a vote?

He shakes his head.

2. An Indian girl.

                    In practice, can you go to the European
                    cinema here?

She shakes her head.

3. An Indian.

                    To hotels?

He shakes his head.

4. An Indian.

                    To bars?

He shakes his head.

5. An Indian girl.

                    Swimming baths?

She shakes her head.

6. An Indian.

                    Public library?

He shakes his head.

29.   DIALOGUE AND ACTION (*continued*)

In the first decade of this century, film producers learned to intercut between pursuer and pursued, and they have been doing it ever since. Every week several dozen filmed series re-enact the ritual—on warehouse catwalk, unfinished building, mountainside. It continues to exert a powerful hold, although it may get more attention from producers than it deserves; the pursuit of criminals is not actually the main problem or pre-occupation of the nation.

The excerpt illustrates an economic point. Various reasons often make it desirable that action sequences of this sort, especially if photographed on location, be done *without sound*. Silent shooting saves time, personnel, and money, and it eliminates the location problems of bad acoustics and the intrusion of irrelevant sounds. Occasionally a producer will want to capitalize on these for a chaotic effect, but more often clarity is preferred. To material shot silently the needed sound elements, including dialogue, music, and selected sounds such as gunfire, can be added later. The dialogue here used involves no synchronization problem; it can be recorded at any time, in any studio. An echo effect can be added by the sound engineer or later by the sound mixer.

To release the camera from inhibitions created by sound problems, producers have in recent years made increasing use of postsynchronization, especially in action sequences. Here the writer has consciously kept postsynchronization problems to a minimum. Frequently used abbreviations: P.O.V. for point of view.

"Family on Trial," by Lawrence Menkin, for series *Code 3*. ABC Films.

66   WIDER ANGLE
     Carl reaches the other building, Purvis after him.
     Now Traube enters the scene, follows the action.

67   INT. SECOND WAREHOUSE
     Carl runs across the open space of the floor,
     looking for cover.

68   INT. SECOND WAREHOUSE - AT ENTRANCE
     Purvis, Traube rush in.

69   CLOSE ON CARL
     Looking desperately for a hiding place.

70   CLOSE ON PURVIS AND TRAUBE
     Looking in the dimly lighted vastness for Carl.

71   MED. CLOSE - AT LADDER
     The ladder leads up to a catwalk. Carl reaches the
     ladder, starts to climb.

72   TWO SHOT - TRAUBE, PURVIS
     They have lost Carl. Exchange looks.

73   CARL - TRAUBE'S AND PURVIS' P.O.V.
     Carl is far up the ladder, now reaches the catwalk,
     is swinging on it.

74   CLOSE SHOT - TRAUBE
     He whips out a flashlight, snaps it on.

75   CARL - ON CATWALK
     As the flashlight beam holds him.

                         TRAUBE'S VOICE
                If you shoot, we'll drop you!
                Take your choice!"

     Carl is frozen by the command.

30.   DIALOGUE AND ACTION (*continued*)

If there is a disparity between the rhythms of speech and the possible rhythms of action, this disparity is most striking in the case of animation. Animation producers are for this reason inclined to be fanatical about eliminating superfluous words. In this 20-second drama, produced in animation, there are twenty-one words, in two sentences. In the middle of the first sentence the wife pauses momentarily for breath, and meanwhile she rushes outside, a teapot floods the house, the husband swims after his wife and catches up to her.

This commercial was presented to its sponsors in "story board" form rather than script form. A story board, resembling a comic strip, is a series of drawings illustrating the key situations, with the dialogue and explanatory text underneath or above. Traditionally, much animation writing has been done by the story board artist, but the television vogue of animation has brought an influx of "typewriter writers."

A "trucking" shot is a shot from a moving camera—a camera "on a truck." Though animation procedure, of course, requires no truck, the terminology hangs on.

"Teatime," 20-second commercial by Playhouse Pictures; storyboard is in John Halas and Roger Manvell, *The Technique of Film Animation.*

1   Teatime in England. Husband and wife are sitting at
    table. Wife pours tea into cup he is holding. In
    background we see a large window.

                    SOUND: FORD MOTOR

    Car zooms by outside.

                         HUSBAND
                    (decided British accent)
                 It's the new Ford...

                         WIFE
                 ...with the most exquisite styling...

    Wife rushes out to see the Ford. The teapot, remain-
    ing in mid-air, continues to pour and fills the entire
    room with tea. Husband, engulfed, swims after her.

2   Wife, teacup in hand, is standing beside Ford "Around
    the World" symbol. Husband arrives dripping wet,
    with teacup still in hand, and joins her beside
    symbol.

                         WIFE
                 ...proved and approved.

                         HUSBAND
                 ...around the world.

                         BOTH
                 See it at your Ford dealer's.

    Truck and pan over to symbol.

31.   DIALOGUE AND ACTION (*continued*)

It has become a standard requirement on many filmed action
series that there be an action "peak" at least every five minutes.
This may involve physical conflict, a beautiful woman, or some
strong new element of suspense, perhaps all three.

The advantage of a scene of the sort here excerpted is clear
enough. It can rivet attention of new viewers even in the middle
of a program. Our private investigator, Mike Hammer, has been
waiting for the mysterious Miss Patti in the hallway of her
apartment house. She arrives late at night, escorted by Stanley.

The television obsession with "strong action" has won severe
criticism. Television is not alone in the obsession, which was
rampant in published fiction, as in the Spillane novels, before
the rise of television. Some argue that the novels are read by
a sedentary group incapable of imitative action, while the programs are watched by the growing young and serve as models for
virile behavior. The arguments are based largely on conjecture.
We know little about the effects of violence in programming. All
we know is that it wins audience response and that producers
and sponsors have vied to satisfy it.

"Death Takes an Encore," adapted by Frank Kane from novelette
Return Engagement, for Mickey Spillane Series. *Revue Productions, Inc.*

                              STANLEY
                    What are you doing here? I told
                    you not to bother Miss Patti.

                               MIKE
                    But I don't understand, I --

                              STANLEY
          Out!

Stanley starts to push him out roughly. Mike is
protesting. Suddenly he whirls. His elbow digs into
Stanley's midsection. As Stanley folds, he tries to
butt Mike. Mike brings the side of his hand down in a
chop. Stanley hits the floor face first. Mike looks
from Stanley to the girl and back.

                               MIKE
                    I'm sorry, Miss Patti. I certainly
                    didn't want to cause all this trouble.
                    I hope I haven't hurt him.

Patti walks over, turns Stanley on his back, looks up
at Mike.

                               PATTI
                    You're quite a man. I never saw anybody
                    take Stanley before. Where d'you learn
                    to handle yourself like that?

32.   DIALOGUE AND ACTION (*continued*)

This excerpt is an example of visual writing, even though it contains a great deal of talk. The continuous talk is there because the scene would be unnatural and embarrassing if it were not. But the talk is largely ritualistic and is not the central interest of the scene. While we take account of what Manley is saying, we are more interested in what he is doing and in the boy's reaction to it. The actions are not startling, but just curious enough to rivet our attention. And the progress of the scene is a product more of the action than of the talk.

The script deals with a high-class reform school for delinquents. A rather well-to-do mother, at wits' end about her son, has just entered him as a pupil. The boy is having his first interview with the headmaster. Naturally, the two, boy and headmaster, are testing each other.

The excerpt suggests that it is not necessarily the avoidance of words, but the meaningful use of action, that is the objective in visual writing.

The Unloved, by Colin Morris, in Michael Barry (ed.), *The Television Playwright.*

Manley lights his pipe, regarding Rolfe narrowly. Then
he turns his back on him, spins his desk chair, and lies
full-length on the divan.

                    MANLEY
          My name's Manley. And that's what they
          call me. We think 'sir' is a bit too
          formal.
                    (with greatest gentleness)
          This must be a frightening experience for
          you. Like to sit down?

Manley waves his hand in the direction of the desk
chair, at which he has carefully closed the file.

          I know when I first went to school, I
          was terrified. I used to lock myself
          in the lavatory for hours on end, to
          keep away from everybody. The first
          night I planned to run away.

He reaches an arm to a table behind him, and picks up
a model plane, and starts the propeller. Rolfe comes
a foot or so nearer the chair, in order to see better.

          Of course, I know all about you. All
          those things that went wrong with the
          police, and the probation officer, and
          the magistrate. I'd like to make it
          clear, Rolfe, that although I know
          everything, no one else does. My wife
          doesn't know, my secretary doesn't know,
          my daughter doesn't know, the staff
          doesn't know and, of course, the boys
          don't know.

He lets the aeroplane fly in Rolfe's direction. Rolfe
brings it back to him.

          Thanks. I think you'd better not tell
          anyone your private affairs. Boys are
          curious and you might <u>feel</u> like telling
          them, but I suggest, for a fortnight at
          least, you say nothing. And at the end
          of that time, I think you'll decide that
          private affairs are private.

Rolfe sits down.

33. NARRATION

That narration plays a larger role in television than in other dramatic media—theatre and theatrical film—has been suggested and illustrated by various excerpts. Most of these (Numbers 7, 9, 12, 17, 18, 20) dealt with on-screen narrators. This and several subsequent excerpts will deal with the frequently used unseen narrator, usually called "off-screen" narrator or "voice-over" narrator.

In launching his *Printer's Measure* with a first-person narrator, Chayefsky creates an identification between the narrator and the camera. The camera movement gives us the narrator's experience of entering the printing shop, as a boy years ago. In a sense the narration is dramatized through this subjective use of the camera. The device is not pursued for its own sake; it is dropped when the boy apprentice pops into view.

A more frequent, more literal procedure would show us the boy himself entering. The variation here used is a stimulating one, especially because it is used sparingly.

Printer's Measure, in Paddy Chayefsky, *Television Plays.*

FADE IN:

A wooden sign swaying ever so little in a May morning
breeze. The sign is old and battered, and the words
"Emperor Press" are barely discernible.

The camera moves slowly down across a store window so
dirty you can hardly see through it...

                         NARRATOR
          In 1939 when I was seventeen years old,
          I went to work in a print shop on West
          Twenty-sixth Street in New York...

The camera moves toward the door, which is one step down
from the sidewalk, opens the door, moves in. We are
faced with a railing that separates the customers from
the shop proper. We push through the swinging door of
the railing and face the shop. It is a crowded, dark,
dank little place. The only illumination is provided
by work bulbs over the stone and over each press...
Between the type cabinets on one wall and the presses
on the other, there is a tortuous passage. The camera
slowly moves down the shop, ducking the moving arm of
the Kluege press.

          My job was to clean the press, fill the
          fountains with ink, a little distributing,
          a little compositing.

At this point the apprentice, who has been bending
down between two presses, suddenly pops into view,
sweeping the floor industriously.

          ...and other duties.

34.   NARRATION (*continued*)

This excerpt illustrates the more usual procedure. During the first-person narration we see the action referred to.

Note that action and narration dovetail but do not echo each other. The narration does not say, "I entered the morgue," since this is shown. The information supplied by the action is effectively confirmed and supplemented by the narration, not duplicated.

The sequence is typical of action series that have a narrative construction. As in the *Dragnet* series (see p. 9), major dialogue scenes are separated by narrative sequences using off-screen narration, often accompanied by a rapid succession of shots having visual variety and movement. In this alternation the dialogue scenes build conflict, the narrative sequences provide a sense of activity and give added information in rapid fashion. The present narrative sequence leads into a fairly substantial dialogue scene in the morgue and morgue antechamber. This would be studio-produced, although some of the shots accompanying narration would be done on location. Note that a shot of Mike entering the morgue building, having been photographed for a previous program, is already available as stock footage in the company's files.

5 EXT. MORGUE. DAY (STOCK)
   Cab drives up, Mike exits cab and enters building.

                         MIKE'S VOICE
                    The morgue is right across the drive
                    from the East River in New York. The
                    occasional hoot of a tug or the clank
                    of its barges doesn't penetrate its
                    thick walls. But even if they did, it
                    wouldn't disturb the deep sleep of its
                    occupants.

6 INT. CORRIDOR. DAY.
   CAMERA FOLLOWS Mike as he walks down the corridor,
   pushes through the door marked "City Morgue."

                         MIKE'S VOICE
                    This is the end of the road for the
                    drifter, the homeless, the accident
                    victim, the tired and forgotten. Here,
                    all are treated alike - the suicide
                    from Beekman Place whose passing rated
                    96-point headlines gets the same accom-
                    modations as the derelict who slept his
                    life away in a Bowery doorway - a slab.
                    That's all they need.

7 INT. ANTECHAMBER TO MORGUE. DAY.
   A thin baldheaded MAN is sitting at a white enameled
   desk. He has a habit of chewing on the cuticle of
   his thumb. He looks up as Mike Hammer approaches
   the desk.

                         ATTENDANT
                    Looking for someone?

35.   NARRATION (*continued*)

The narration in this excerpt was an ad-lib creation, obtained through interview. The technique was briefly discussed on p. 10.

The program deals with the actual case of a boy charged with murder, on doubtful evidence. The dramatic features of the case, as brought out in the program, were the role of the New York police in suppressing evidence that cast doubt on the boy's guilt, and the role of the communication media in assuming his guilt and ignoring the findings that cast doubt on it.

CBS-TV interviewed the boy at length about his experience. This filmed and recorded material was used in various ways. In the present excerpt, portions of the sound track are used as an off-screen narration, accompanied by film, shot in the places referred to. We see no people in these shots. But we move down the tunnel as Maceri must have done en route to his cell. We therefore get a subjective-camera feeling, similar to that produced in excerpt Number 33.

Edward R. Murrow, who completed the program before he left CBS-TV to head the United States Information Agency, explains on the air how and when the filmed material was obtained. Some producers might fear this would "spoil the illusion." It does not; it adds to the integrity of the presentation.

"A Real Case of Murder: The People vs. Peter Maceri," by CBS News staff, for *CBS Reports*.

                              MURROW
        The court sent Maceri to the Brooklyn
        House of Detention, a maximum security
        prison...This was Peter Maceri's first
        taste of prison. After he described it
        to us we filmed the interior.

CUT TO:

Film sequence, Brooklyn House of Detention. Camera
moves through tunnel, etc.

                              PETER
        You go down through a tunnel - across the
        street, handcuffed - and they fingerprint
        you and take mugshots of you. Then they
        make you sit in a cell until maybe about
        a quarter after nine - then they take you
        up on an elevator - then they bring you
        to a floor - and you have a little orange
        card with your fingerprint and a picture
        of you and with the cell number on it that
        they had assigned to you. And he looks
        at it, and he says, "You're in this here
        location - and this is your cell." And
        they lock you in - and they closed the
        steel doors behind me. That's what gave
        me - then I had to sit down on my bed,
        thinking for a little while - and then I
        decided I couldn't stay up no more. I
        was getting tired because I didn't sleep
        for two days. I couldn't believe, yet,
        when I woke up in the morning - looking
        out at the bars - and that's all that you
        could see was two - two - one, your bars,
        and then another set of bars - and then
        these thick windows. I felt lost at times.
        I knew - I figured if it went this far
        with me, I'd probably get the electric
        chair. I'd probably get time for something
        I didn't do - and it was getting me nervous.

36. TRANSITION

Sooner or later the writer has the problem of moving his action from one setting to another. He is expected to indicate what sort of transition he proposes. This is because the choice of transition has a bearing on the structure and rhythm of the program.

His alternatives begin with the simplest and swiftest device, the cut, a direct jump from one scene to another. It appears in the script as "CUT TO." In film practice this appears on a line by itself, usually at the extreme right (Number 37) although some companies place it at the left (Number 35). In live television the phrase is also generally placed on a line by itself, but some writers may embed the direction in a paragraph, as here shown.

The cut is, of course, used within scenes as well as between scenes. Within a scene we may jump from long shot to medium shot to close-up, or to a reverse-angle shot, or some other kind of shot, and such jumps are usually done via the simple cut. Since this is the normal practice within any scene or action sequence, the words "CUT TO" are not used for such jumps (see Number 29). But when jumping to an entirely new setting, a new sequence of action, a method of transition is specified.

In the present transition, the two scenes are continuous in time and subject matter, and there is, therefore, every reason to use the simplest and most direct transition. The close relationship of the scenes is emphasized by the continuation, in the second scene, of the sound background of the first scene.

Old MacDonald Had a Curve, in *Patterns: Four Television Plays.*

He throws another, stops, listens to their laughter.

                    MAC
          An' the day I can't beat a bunch of old
          men, I'll just go get me buried some place.

Throws with tremendous effort.

We CUT TO a shot of the infirmary, Carol looking out of
the window. Doctor sits on a stool reading a chart.
The sounds of the horseshoe game are audible through
the window.

                    DOCTOR
          I think we better put Mr. Huber back on a
          salt-free diet. I don't like the looks of
          his pressure. Carol...

                    CAROL
          Mr. Huber?

                    DOCTOR
          What's so interesting out the window?
          You've been standing there for ten minutes.

                    CAROL
          They pick on old Mr. MacDonald so much

                    DOCTOR
                    (grins)
          Old Mr. MacDonald invites it. He sends out
          engraved invitations for collective ribbings
          six nights a week. Ever hear the old guy
          talk about his baseball experiences? That's
          six pages out of Ripley.

                    CAROL
          But he was a pitcher.

                    DOCTOR
          Sure he was - fifty years ago. Darn good,
          too. And that's not just my opinion.
                    (laughingly)
          That's his, too.

37.   TRANSITION (*continued*)

The cut may or may not involve a lapse of time. It does not, in itself, make any implication as to time. The eye sees the change of place, but the change of time must be defined by content, if it is necessary to define it.

In the previous example the continuation of the sound background, and dialogue references, led us promptly to assume that time was continuous. In the present example we would know, if we thought about it, that time is not continuous. But there is really no need for thinking about it. What happens in the first scene produces the action seen in the second. How long it takes for MacDonald to get to the phone booth is irrelevant. The author wants abruptness and gets it through "CUT TO."

MacDonald, famous pitcher of decades ago, is in an old-men's home. A sudden peculiar knot in his shoulder has caused him to start throwing extraordinary curves with a horseshoe, and then with a baseball. He rejoins the Brooklyn team in the big leagues. But his comeback is ruined because the peculiar knot disappears, apparently in response to the attention he has received from the team's trainers. Now he goes back to the old-men's home, deflated. In our excerpt, the final action of the play, we have put the words "CUT TO" in the normal film position.

Old MacDonald Had a Curve.

> DOCTOR
> Well, now the excitement's over. It was
> fun while it lasted - but just between you
> and me, I'm glad we're back to normal!

And as he says this a horseshoe flies through the
window, landing on the same shelf. The doctor rushes
to the window.

> DOCTOR
> What fool threw that?

> VOICE (off)
> MacDonald!

> DOCTOR
> Oh, nooooo! You mean - ?

> VOICE (off)
> Yep. Got his curve back!

CUT TO:

PHONE BOOTH. Door closing. MacDonald on the phone.

> MAC
> New York City?...I wanna person-to-person
> talk with Leo Durocher...That's right. This
> is Firebrand Lefty MacDonald...

38.   TRANSITION (*continued*)

The fact that cuts from one place to another can involve jumps in time of which we are not conscious can lend extraordinary speed and zest to a sequence like the one here excerpted. The jumps are to different parts of a multiple-part set and show how a set of this sort provides flexibility in the use of time.

In this episode Ozzie and Harriet have the impression that David is about to get married in a hasty wedding at the office of the justice of the peace.

The Adventures of Ozzie and Harriet, by Don Nelson, Jay Sommers, Ozzie Nelson, Dick Bensfield, Perry Grant; in *Best Television Humor.*

                    OZZIE
          If we hurry we can get there in time to
          stop them...Let's go! Where are my pants?

     Harriet tosses them in. He gets into them in one
     jump.

19   HALL, LIVING ROOM, DINING ROOM, KITCHEN
     Harriet and Ozzie tearing downstairs, rush through
     house to backyard, Ozzie stopping at closet to grab
     his jacket.

20   BACKYARD
     Harriet and Ozzie rush across the yard to the garage
     door. Ozzie stops and searches his pockets...

                    HARRIET
          What's the matter?

                    OZZIE
          My car keys! They must be upstairs!

     He rushes back into the house.

                    HARRIET
          Ozzie!

21   BEDROOM

                    OZZIE
                 (appearing at window)
          I'm looking for the keys.

22   BACKYARD

                    HARRIET
          The keys are in the car. Come on, hurry
          up! It's twenty-five after...

23   BEDROOM WINDOW
     Ozzie starts to climb out window.

                    HARRIET (O.S.)
          No, no, no. Use the stairs!

39.   TRANSITION (*continued*)

In this excerpt the various transitions might have been done with cuts rather than dissolves, without any loss of clarity to the audience. Time relationships are not altered in any way by the use of dissolves instead of cuts. To the extent that time relationships are important, they must be made clear by dialogue or other means.

In a dissolve one scene fades out while the new scene fades in, so that there is an overlap of the two. The writer may ask for a fast dissolve or a slow dissolve; the overlap may be anywhere from a fraction of a second to a number of seconds.

A factor arguing for dissolves in this sequence is the repetitive nature of the shots. The lady keeps staring, the plane flying, the traffic moving, the hotel standing. None of these actions ends at a particular moment, and if a cut were used, the moment of its occurrence would be arbitrary. The series of dissolves gives the sequence a constant feeling of change. There is always something happening in a dissolve. A series of cuts would probably seem slower in this sequence, even if the same amount of time were used.

The stock shots used here are of the sort that can be purchased from a stock shot library. "East to west" means, of course, right to left; film and television subscribe to the map maker's convention in this respect.

"King's Ransom," by Steven Thornley, for series *Meet McGraw.* M. M., Inc.

                              MRS. LEAR
                    What you trying to say, mister?

McGraw starts to answer, then thinks better of it.

                              MCGRAW
                    Nothing.

He picks up his briefcase and hat...As McGraw goes
to the door, opening it, he turns and looks back at
the old woman, again staring into space. He goes
out.

                                          DISSOLVE TO:

16   EXT. AIRLINER - DAY (STOCK)
     It is in flight, east to west.

                                          DISSOLVE TO:

17   EXT. CITY OF LOS ANGELES - DAY (STOCK)
     Any self-identifying shot will do.

                                          DISSOLVE TO:

18   INT. LOBBY MED. LONG SHOT - MCGRAW, OTHERS - DAY
     The shot is angled from the desk toward the entrance
     as McGraw and the bellhop enter.

40.   TRANSITION (*continued*)

This excerpt illustrates a third type of transition: the FADE-OUT followed by a FADE-IN. The directions are here placed in their most usual position.

This device differs from the dissolve in that there is no overlap. There may or may not be an interval of dark screen between the fade-out and the fade-in, but in any case there is a sense of waiting. This may be fatal unless the transition comes at a moment of strong suspense, in which case it may sharpen the suspense. The fade-out followed by the fade-in is generally used only between major portions of the story. In the present instance some might prefer a dissolve.

The set used in this sequence is a multiple-part set. It shows a drawing room and an adjoining outside area at the elegant Hinks home in Georgia in 1861. The first scene shows a lavish ball at its height; the next is after the ball. This is the kind of transition achieved on the stage by a lowering of lights. In television, the beginner is attracted to a parallel device: a fade-out of the ballroom during the ball, followed by a fade-in of the same room after the ball. But this is likely to be a dull transition, putting the burden on clichés of change, like clocks, filled ash trays, and half-empty glasses. The excerpt shows how easily a multiple-part set solves the problem. At the height of the ball we have followed the older brother outside, where his younger brother is making love. It is from this outdoor spot that the transition is made. The point: the best way to make a change of time is to make a change of place simultaneously.

Honor, by Gore Vidal; in *Television Plays for Writers.*

                        GRAYSON
            Little brother...

                        AARON
            Little brother's going to crack your
            head if you don't go away.

                        GRAYSON
                        (amused)
            Miss Amelia, beware of this sinister
            cadet who writes poems.

Grayson goes.

                        AMELIA
                        (dreamily)
            Tell me a poem.

                        AARON
            "Darkling, I listen and for many a time
            I have been half in love with easeful death..."

                        AMELIA
            That's sad.

Aaron kisses her, suddenly intense.

                        AARON
            Girl...girl, darlin' girl!

                                        FADE OUT

FADE IN:

The drawing room; the party is over. Minna puts out
the candles as Hinks in shirt sleeves enters from the
hall.

41. REAR PROJECTION

Various excerpts have illustrated usage of stock footage, also known as "library footage." In several excerpts the footage was used briefly for a scene-setting purpose. In the present excerpt footage again serves a scenic purpose, but as a continuing background via rear projection. A shot using rear projection is called a "process shot" in film usage.

The excerpt illustrates the possible virtuosity of the technique. The carriage, jolting rhythmically, stands in front of a rear-projection screen on which the moving background is projected. At first the screen is beside the carriage and the background travels across the screen. But in the final shot the screen is behind the carriage and a receding background is used.

"Die by the Gun," story by Lawrence Menkin, teleplay by Christopher Knopf, for series *Wanted—Dead or Alive*. Four Star Films, Inc., and Malcolm Productions, Inc.

CAMERA TRAVELING with the stage as it proceeds at
good pace along road. In driver's seat sits Nebro.

                    NEBRO
          (singing, a painful thing to hear)
       The hick that threw the brick,
       He will never throw another,
       For calling me a son of a bear
       he now lies under cover...

11 INT. STAGE (PROCESS) - DAY
    Nebro's singing coming over. Joe, edgy enough as it
    is, reacts to it, angrily.

                    NEBRO'S VOICE
                 (the song continuing)
       And above his head these words are read,
       You can see them if you rubber:
       "Here lies the hick that threw the brick,
       He'll never throw another..."

                    JOE
          Can't you shut him up!

    Josh glances at Joe, then sticks head out the window.

                    JOSH
          Hey, Nebro!

12 EXT. NEBRO IN DRIVER'S SEAT (PROCESS) - DAY
    as shot from front of stage, FULL ON NEBRO. He
    turns, looks back at Josh in bg.

                    JOSH
          Lay off the moose call, will you?

                    NEBRO
          Moose call!!...I'll have you know...

                    JOSH
          (eyes widening at something ahead)
          Nebro, look out!

42.   REAR PROJECTION (*continued*)

Rear projection also can make use of still photographs, as in this excerpt.

Line drawings, engravings, and other kinds of graphic art have also been used as rear-projected backgrounds, sometimes with stunning and stimulating effect. Comedy, variety, and dance programs have been more experimental in this respect than drama programs.

The excerpt also illustrates how effectively television, when it wishes, can rise above literalism. The appearance of Jack Paar in the corner of the screen, apparently in a split-screen effect, to speak his "English subtitles," is a pleasantly fanciful use of a device more generally used for phone calls.

Jack Paar Show, by Sidney Reznick, Bob Howard, Jack Paar, Larry Markes. In *Best Television Humor.*

                         JACK
          After analyzing the claims of one shady
          used-car salesman, I have reached the
          point where I can interpret the true
          meaning behind what is said. Let's listen
          to a fictitious used-car dealer...I'll
          furnish the English subtitles.

CUT TO Nye in vest before rear-projection of car-lot.
Talks directly to camera, and Jack is seen in corner
of screen.

                         NYE
          Yes, sir, I spotted you the minute you
          walked on the lot...I said, "Now there's
          my kind of people.

                         JACK
          He means, "Hello sucker."

                         NYE
          I've got just the car in mind for you,
          friend. It's big and roomy and comfortable.
          Tell you the truth, I hate to see it go;
          I use it myself.

                         JACK
          As an office.

                         NYE
          Here it is, friend, and if you like it, I
          advise you to strike now - while the iron
          is hot.

                         JACK
          It just came out of the soldering shop.

                         NYE
          There she is...Yes sir, that's a real honey.

                         JACK
          Yes, sir, real honey. If you look underneath
          you can see it dripping from the crankcase.

43. MODELS

This excerpt is an approximate reconstruction of the opening of a CBS-TV documentary program. The subject was Tibet.

Since television sees with one eye at a time, we cannot judge the size of things seen. That which fills the screen may be four miles or four inches wide. The model in this case, introduced by a succession of film shots, was instantly accepted as a vast plateau ringed by mountains. Only when a hand reached into the set did one see that it was a model. The virtue of the device is that, once the vastness and remoteness of the terrain have been established, it reduces these to proportions that permit observation and discussion.

An opposite procedure might deal, to similar effect, with microscopic material. We see a microscope. Then we see what the microscope sees, a magnification of a drop of water. Then we dissolve to a larger magnification of the same thing—on a huge rear-projection screen, although we do not know this. Then a man steps in front of a corner of the screen, to discuss and point out details. The smallness of the man will in this case be as much of a shock as was the hugeness of the hand in the other sequence. Again trickery has achieved a practical goal: a guided tour through the microscopic.

Adventure. CBS-TV with co-operation of Museum of Natural History.

FADE IN:

Film. Distant shot of mountains surrounding Tibet.
Peaks lost in clouds.

DISSOLVE TO:

Film. A closer shot of same mountains, from an
airplane.

DISSOLVE TO:

Film. A still closer aerial shot, from a higher point.
Through a break in the clouds we glimpse a high plateau
beyond the peaks.

DISSOLVE TO:

Model. We are looking down onto the plateau from one
side of the ring of peaks. We move toward the plateau.

COLLINGWOOD
There lies Tibet...

His hand enters the frame, pointing. Camera tilts up
to bring him into frame, standing behind the model.

44. GRAPHIC MATERIAL

Still pictures reach the television screen through a variety of technical means. The still picture one sees on the small, luminous screen may have been rear-projected in the studio. Or it may have been photographed on an easel, by a studio camera. Or, in the case of live television, it may originate in a slide projector or opaque projector. The "telop," an opaque projector designed for television, projects stills approximately 4 by 5 inches in size. It is generally mounted in the same room as the film projectors. A succession of stills can be incorporated into a program at any time from the telop.

The excerpt illustrates a typical effect. Several fictional head-lines have been reproduced on telop cards and, on cue, are super-imposed over other material—in this case, footage of major-league baseball.

The television writer is not concerned with the mechanics in-volved, but he should be aware that it is possible in a live tele-cast, at comparatively little cost, to use a rapid succession of stills.

Old MacDonald Had a Curve.

FADE IN:

Film clip of a major-league baseball game.

SUPERIMPOSE:

 Headline, "Aged Pitcher Signs with Brooklyn."
 Clear for -

 Variety headline, "Flatbush Fetches Fossil
 Flinger." Clear for -

 Headline, "You're Only as Old as You Feel, Says
 Maxwell MacDonald." Clear for -

 Time Magazine cover, his picture with caption
 "Old Man of the Year." Clear and -

Hold clip a few seconds

DISSOLVE TO:

"On the Air" sign in a studio. Tilt down for shot of
announcer on a sportcast.

ANNOUNCER

   And that brings us, friends, to our
   sports spotlight - which in turn only
   naturally takes us to Brooklyn.

45.   GRAPHIC MATERIAL (*continued*)

A memorable use of the graphic arts was included in the magnificent Shakespeare series of the British Broadcasting Corporation, *An Age of Kings*. A special tapestry incorporated all the major characters of the Shakespearean cycle of chronicle plays. Each program began with a panning movement across this tapestry, across centuries of history. The camera eventually centered on the main character of the individual program. The tapestry texture, rarely seen on television, contributed to the arresting quality of the effect.

The texture of period material was used in a somewhat different way by a BBC dramatist to introduce, in a surprising fashion, the story of a touring American lady. This excerpt presents the opening moments.

The producers of sponsored programs are too inclined to be wary of nonliving materials. They have faith in the dramatic attraction of people, not of things. But here the juxtaposition of the nonliving and the living creates instant drama.

Mrs. Wickens in the Fall, by Nigel Kneale; in Michael Barry (ed.), *The Television Playwright.*

FADE IN:

INT. CORRIDOR. DAY.

C.S. of a French medieval tapestry. It shows armoured
knights in combat, the lance of one transfixing the
other.

Crash in music at full volume. Horns predominate.

The camera cranes downwards from the tapestry, past
tattered banners and a set-piece of swords and daggers
fixed on a bare stone wall. Down to the helmet of a
suit of armour, so that it suddenly fills the frame:
the visor is up, and the black interior cavity faces
camera.

After a moment a hand comes into shot and touches the
dark metal, exploring cautiously.

The music enters a quieter phase.

The camera pulls back to take in the owner of the hand
...a mild-faced American woman in her early sixties.
Her clothes are new but not expensive -- a new vacation
outfit, chosen in the staider stores of a small Mid-
western town. Her shoulder-bag dangles. As she looks
up at the helmet, her face is pinched with what seems
to be the effort of concentration.

                                        SUPERIMPOSE:

    Main Title

46. GRAPHIC MATERIAL (*continued*)

In an industry too inclined to literalness, it is pleasant to come across a triumphant though unpretentious use of a non-literal approach. To many advertisers it might seem that a boy eating a piece of bread with gusto would have far more impact than a piece of bread without a boy. Yet here we have the piece of bread being eaten, and the boy is not shown. The presumably wholesome grin, teeth and freckles have all been omitted. Instead we have the stimulus of the incomplete statement, which the audience must complete.

This is simple animation at its most simplified.

Commercial in simple animation, for Levy's Rye.

FADE IN:

CU, a slice of rye bread, filling screen.

After a moment, a bite-sized piece of the bread,
rounded as by a bite, suddenly disappears. Then
another piece disappears from another part of the
slice. Then another and another, rapidly, until
slice is gone.

                    NARRATOR
                    (meanwhile)

          It's mouth-watering...All New York
          is eating it up...

As the bite-sized pieces vanish, some block letters
are partially revealed, on surface behind slice. As
slice disappears in five or six bites, the word LEVY
is seen.

                    NARRATOR
                    (continuing)
          ...Levy's Rye.

47. GRAPHIC MATERIAL (*continued*)

In this more complex animation sequence we have a glimpse
of the truly visual writer at work. The film was cosponsored
by the United Nations, ten of its specialized agencies and the
National Educational Television and Radio Center. It was designed and written by an artist-writer.

Exemplifying the concentration with which animation can
do its work, he brings into interrelationship within a few seconds three vast areas of subject matter. The unifying device, a
visual motif, is startling in its simplicity and directness. The
writer is here writing mainly with his drawing pencil; what it
says is supplemented, in very sparing manner, by the spoken
word.

Water, by Philip Stapp. Center for Mass Communication, of Columbia
University Press.

Animated sequence of water in motion, changing form, changing direction.

                        NARRATOR
            Water!...water everywhere...above the
            earth...across the earth...beneath the
            earth.

MUSIC: SUDDEN BRILLIANT FLOURISH

A pattern springs up: a trunk branching out into many branches, which then sprout leaves, revealing the pattern as that of a tree.

            Water, essential to all life...

                                          FADE OUT

FADE IN:

Starting at the upper part of the frame, with small lines coming together in larger and larger branches, the same pattern forms, identically placed in the frame, but this time we see it as a great river fed by its tributaries.

            Always on the move...

                                          FADE OUT

FADE IN:

The same pattern takes shape, but this time, as detail and texture are added, we see it as a system of arteries in the human body.

            Water inside us...

                                          FADE OUT

48.   GRAPHIC MATERIAL (*continued*)

Pursuing bypaths of animation, we have arrived at a point
where animator and historian meet. This excerpt is considered
animation because of the way the material is used (see pp.
14–16).

In the use of still pictures, an important factor in many
sequences is an exactly computed movement of camera in relation to picture, bringing to attention the right detail at the
right moment, in juxtaposition to precisely the right words and
musical moments. Camera movements have not been included
in the quoted excerpt because they would mean little without
reference to each of the pictures. But several of the effects can
be explained.

Item 61 was a map that showed the alternative routes available at one place to the wagon trains: a mountain route and a
desert route. The camera made an east-west pan across this
map. This movement was carried through in a number of the
landscape scenes following. A pan across one desert scene was
sometimes continued in the next, with a linking dissolve. In the
case of Item 63, this movement brought into the frame, at the
words, "Death had a few extra hands," a small gravestone
marked KILLED BY INDIANS, surrounded by a crude, improvised
fence. Item 67 brought into view an astonishing sight. A pan
across empty desert arrived suddenly at an ornate double bed
and an easy chair, abandoned in mid-journey.

The narrator, Gary Cooper, handled all spoken words including quotations from letters and diaries. With a less celebrated narrator, such quotations might have been assigned to
other "voices."

The Real West, by Philip Reisman, Jr. NBC-TV Special Projects Unit.

#61

NARRATOR

But if there was danger in the mountains,
there was no safety at sea level.

#62

One traveler wrote of the desert trails...
"It was as though the hand of Death had
been laid upon the country."

#63

Where it was Apache country...Death had
a few extra hands.

#64

"We have just learned that the party ahead
of us has nearly perished of thirst...

#65

...and there is one behind us carrying the
smallpox...

#66

...It is more than one hundred degrees in
the heat...Truly we are traversing Hell
with the fires banked...

#67

...it is milestoned with what once were
precious belongings...but such sentiments
are too burdensome for exhausted horses."

#68

"Our map promised that at this place we
would find good grass and water. But it
lied. The grass was poisonous and the
spring was dry..."

#69

Another company traveled eighty miles
without water...then almost drowned in
a cloudburst. Their stock stampeded and
their wagons, the wood desiccated in the
heat, fell apart.

49.   SOUND AND MUSIC

In television, sound effects are seldom called on to do more than supply the expected sounds of trains, traffic, airplanes, hoofs, stagecoach wheels, babbling brooks, gunfire and ringing telephones, although sound effects have been the subject of considerable experimentation in radio and in various periods of film history. Occasionally television remembers this experimentation and makes use of nonliteral sound effects, for comic or expressionist reasons, or both.

In this sequence Jack Benny has been talking with Frances Bergen, wife of the ventriloquist Edgar Bergen. Charlie McCarthy, the ventriloquist's dummy, has made a brief appearance and Frances has sent him to get a clean necktie. Benny is astounded.

The Jack Benny Show, in *Best Television Humor.*

                              JACK
               Frances...that was Charlie McCarthy!
               He's real! All these years...all these
               years I thought he was a dummy.

                              FRANCES
               Jack, you're kidding.

                              JACK
               No, I'm not.

                              FRANCES
               You've been in show business all your life.
               How could you be so naive?

                              JACK
               I don't know...I don't know...I just can't
               believe it.

Jack sits down, weakly. Charlie re-enters holding a
tie between his fingers.

                              CHARLIE
               How is this one, Mrs. Bergen?

                              FRANCES
               Fine, fine. Let me tie it for you.

While Frances ties Charlie's tie, Jack looks at him,
fingers Charlie's shoulder, then puts his hand up under
his coat.

                              CHARLIE
               Are you trying to pick my pocket?

                              JACK
               No, no, I just straightened your coat.

Jack sits down. Knocks on table, then knocks on
Charlie's head. No sound. Then Jack knocks on his
own head.

               SOUND: OF KNOCK ON WOOD

50.   SOUND AND MUSIC (*continued*)

In this imaginative excerpt from a Jack Paar sketch, the writer does with music something akin to what the Jack Benny excerpt did with a sound effect. The present excerpt is based on the fact that television is one-eared. Earlier (Number 43) we saw an experiment based on the fact that television is, similarly, one-eyed. Such supposed limitations prove, again and again, to be fruitful.

This sequence was introduced with the comment that nothing is more annoying around the house than a mysterious sound that you can't locate. To stop the sound of dripping from a tap, for example, you may have to shut off six faucets. "Where to look for these annoyances has always been a problem. Tonight we'd like to present this problem, together with some suggestions of places you probably haven't thought of. . . ."

The Jack Paar Show, sketch by Earle Doud.

Paar in living room set. Writing at desk.

MUSIC: SNEAK IN 'CHILDREN'S MARCHING SONG'

Paar looks up, slightly annoyed. Slowly gets up. Goes
over and slams the door.

MUSIC: OUT

He goes back to writing. After a moment:

MUSIC: IN AGAIN

He looks up. Slowly gets up and slams window shut.

MUSIC: OUT

He goes back to writing. After a moment:

MUSIC: IN AGAIN

Slowly gets up, goes and slams bureau drawers shut.

MUSIC: OUT

He goes back to writing. After a moment:

MUSIC: IN AGAIN

Slowly gets up. Confused. Takes rifle. Goes to moose
head on wall. Sticks barrel in moose mouth.

SOUND: SHOT
MUSIC: OUT

Waits. Not hearing anything, returns to writing. Then:

MUSIC: IN AGAIN

Angrily gets up. Looks around. Sees picture of Mona
Lisa. Tearing off a piece of adhesive tape from roll
on desk, he goes over and tapes up Mona Lisa's mouth.

MUSIC: OUT

51.   SOUND AND MUSIC (*continued*)

That music can interpret, more richly than realistic sound, the steady dripping of water that through the ages has built astonishing forms and figures in the Carlsbad Caverns of New Mexico, need not surprise anyone. Music composed for the motion picture has often shown its power to prod the imagination. The surprise is to find such music appearing on a live, journalistic program. *Wide, Wide World* took the viewer each Sunday to a wide range of places, using often sixty or seventy cameras ranged throughout the continent, and jumping casually from a festival in Vancouver, British Columbia, to a pirogue race in the Mississippi bayou country, to an underground cavern in New Mexico. Camera action was planned in advance, along with words to go with it. And the writer could, if he wished, commandeer music.

Wide Wide World, NBC-TV staff.

King's Chamber.
CU, drops dripping from stalactite.

MUSIC: BACK SCENE WITH MUSICAL DRIPS

                        GARROWAY
...The climate of the earth shifted a tiny
bit, and it rained up above. And the water
worked its way down through the cracks,
drop by drop, to the ceiling of the caves.

MUSICAL DRIP

A drop of rain quivered on a jagged
piece of ceiling.

MUSICAL DRIP

Sometimes the water evaporated before it
could fall, and a tiny speck of lime was
left behind.

MUSICAL DRIP CONTINUES

Sometimes the drops fell quickly to the
cavern floor, and left the speck of lime
there.

Camera begins to dolly. Pan right.

Drop by drop, speck by speck, the stalactites
grew downward from the ceiling. Speck by
speck the stalagmites piled up on the floors
of the caves...Small formations grew large
in a hundred thousand years. In two hundred
thousand years, the stony icicles hanging
from the ceiling joined with the ones growing
up from the floor, joined and...

52. CLIMAX

Hour after hour, as millions watch, programs reach their climaxes. The climax reveals what we are up to. In every climax an attitude is implicit, if not explicit.

The climax here illustrated is perhaps the basic climax of American television in the early years of its second decade. Philip Marlowe, the leading character, has pursued his investigation to the point where he has the goods on someone. There was a period in the drama of investigation when this would have been sufficient. A court of law would sift the evidence; and the guilty, it is understood, would be punished. But the unmasking of wrong has become tame and is now a mere preliminary. The essential thing is that the guilty man must now attempt escape and/or violence and that, after a brutal combat, Marlowe will triumph. The implication seems to be that any issue must ultimately be settled on the basis of fist, knife, or gun. Or perhaps the main implication is that we need not worry, that good men are always stronger and tougher fighters than bad men. Are these twin implications, hammered out a hundred times a week, unconscious reflections of an armament-race era? Or are they merely reflections of a merchandising system that must sell virility because it must sell beer, cigars, automobiles, vitamins, deodorants, whisky and tooth paste in larger quantities? Perhaps the hindsight of a later decade will tell us more.

"Mother Dear," by James Moser, for series *Philip Marlowe*. Bilmar Productions.

                              CHICO
                    I don't have it here. I keep it some
                    other place.

Quickly Marlowe sweeps his drink aside, reaches out and
grabs Chico by the shirt front, pulls him hard against
the bar.

                              MARLOWE
                    Good boy, Chico. You're a quick study.

                              CHICO
                           (frightened)
                    What do you want?

                              MARLOWE
                    Let me try a couple of names on you.
                    Senora Sandoval...

                              CHICO
                           (reacts, frightened)
                    I don't know her...

                              MARLOWE
                    Ramon Sandoval.

                              CHICO
                    You're mixed up, Senor...

                              MARLOWE
                    I got you cold, Chico. C'mon, unload.

Chico makes a sudden break for a rear door but Marlowe
catches up with him, spins him around. Chico knees
him viciously, delivers two hard smashes on the face,
turns again to escape but Marlowe hangs on. The battle
continues. At one point Chico breaks free, draws a
switchblade. Marlowe finally disarms him and the fight
winds up with Chico flat on his face near one end of
the bar. Marlowe pulls him to his feet, pushes him
hard against the bar.

                              MARLOWE
                    All right, amigo. It's story time. Give!

53.   CLIMAX (*continued*)

There are, of course, exponents of less violent fare; and these have shown that they too can hold large audiences. An example of their success is *Leave It to Beaver,* a series that presents, without a rigid plot pattern, the very nonviolent experiences of a likable, rather average American family. It finds its plot material in the commonest ethical crises of suburbia and often manages to surprise its audiences with scenes and situations that are very close to home. In this episode the family has been planning excitedly for a gala outing. The occasion will be the Saturday track meet, at which Wally Cleaver will run for his school. But there is catastrophe. There is towel throwing in the locker room and Wally is provoked into retaliating just when the coach comes in; the coach suspends Wally from the team. The injustice rankles; it was Eddie and Lumpy who started it, and they will run. Beaver, the younger brother, stays hopeful. "Hey, maybe ten minutes before the bus leaves for Lynnwood, Eddie and Lumpy will come runnin' up and say, 'Coach, we couldn't keep quiet any longer—we did it!' And then the coach will put you on the bus and you'll go to Lynnwood and in the last second you'll win the whole meet." It happens every week, Beaver tells them, on *Men of Annapolis.* Miraculously, Eddie and Lumpy do come forward and confess. And Beaver assumes —along with the audience, we can be sure—that everything will now be all right. The characters include Ward, the father, and June, the mother.

"Wally's Track Meet," by Joe Connelly and Robert Mosher, for series *Leave It to Beaver.* Gomalco Productions, Inc.

                            BEAVER
Boy, it's gonna be neat. We'll go up to the
meet and eat Mom's sandwiches and potato
salad and watch Wally skunk Lynnwood.

                             WARD
Well, not so fast, Beaver. This doesn't take
Wally off the hook. It just means that Lumpy
and Eddie aren't going either.

                            BEAVER
But gee whiz, they started the whole towel
fight and everything.

                             WARD
Yes, but Wally threw the towels too.

                            BEAVER
Yeah, but it was self-defense. Like on
television, if some guy draws on you first,
you can blow his head off and everyone pats
you on the back and tells you what a neat
guy you are.

                             WARD
Well, I know it may be hard for you to believe,
but life isn't exactly like television.

                             JUNE
That's right. Wally shouldn't have thrown
the towels back at the other boys.

                            WALLY
But I got so sore I couldn't help it.

                             WARD
You've just got to learn not to let people
get you that mad. Because what you do is
your own responsibility, no matter why you
do it.

3. A Business Portfolio

3. A Business Portfolio

GUILD

Most television writers belong to the Writers Guild of America, which also includes screen and radio writers. It is organized in two branches:

> Writers Guild of America, East, Inc.
> 22 West 48th Street
> New York 36, New York

> Writers Guild of America, West, Inc.
> 8955 Beverly Boulevard
> Los Angeles 48, California

The Guild acts as a union representing writers in the above fields, in collective bargaining. It also checks individual contracts, prepares occasional market reports and other informational material for its members, organizes craft meetings, and studies copyright, censorship, and tax problems affecting the writer. Special projects of the Guild have included establishment of a pension fund, a credit union, and group insurance for members.

GUILD CONTRACTS

In the television field, the Guild has made agreements with the major networks, film companies, and other program producers, specifying minimum conditions for the employment of writers. There are contracts covering various kinds of staff writers, including news writers, in the principal television centers, and others covering free-lance writers. The free-lance contracts include a *live-television* agreement, a *television-film* agreement, and a *documentary-television-film* agreement. Certain kinds of writing—for instance, "material written by government employees, acting within the scope of their government employment"—are excluded from coverage. But most writing done for network or filmed television in the United States is covered by these "minimum basic agreements."

The live-television agreement states that the company will not employ any writer for work covered by the agreement

> on terms and conditions less favorable to the Employee than those set forth in this Agreement. Only the Union and the Company shall have the right to waive any of the provisions of this Agreement . . .

The term "Employee" in this context means free-lance writer. (See pp. 18–20 for the background of this.)

The clause just quoted means that the individual writer is automatically protected, by this and other minimum basic agreements, from substandard terms. This is true whether or not he is already a Guild member. Moreover, the terms are minimum:

> Nothing in this Agreement . . . shall prevent an Employee from negotiating or obtaining better terms than the minimums herein provided.

The television-film agreements employ almost identical wording.

The various basic agreements are bulky documents. For example, the live-television agreement covers ninety-six mimeographed pages, single spaced. Much of this is in legal language. Points of major interest to the free-lance writer, especially the beginning writer, will be outlined in this section. We shall deal particularly with matters relating to single programs, or to scripts, complete in themselves, telecast on anthology series. Other kinds of series, especially those written under term contracts, are more likely to concern the well-established writer.

GUILD MEMBERSHIP

One television script produced, or a contract to write a television script, qualifies the writer for membership in the Guild.

No one needs to be a member to place his first script. But the nonmember must apply for membership within thirty days after employment begins. With minor qualifications, each of the companies signing the live-television agreement agrees that it

> will employ as Employees covered by this Agreement, and maintain in its employment as such Employees, only such persons as are members of the Union in good standing or shall make application for such membership within thirty (30) days after the date of employment hereunder.

The film agreements have parallel clauses. In other words, the television writing field is with minor exceptions covered by a "guild shop." This differs from a closed shop in that the Guild agrees to admit to membership anyone engaged by a company to write for television. In fact, the Guild pledges that it

> will promptly admit to membership . . . any person whom the Company may hereafter employ as an Employee within the coverage of this Agreement upon the same terms and conditions (including the payment of initiation fees and membership dues) as are uniformly required by the Union as a condition of acquiring or retaining membership.

The Guild pledges in the minimum basic agreements that it will not set up any membership requirements which discriminate

> because of sex, race, creed, color, national origin or previous employment.

In some unions, the entry of new talent has been made difficult by astronomical initiation fees. In some unions of the entertainment field, the initiation fee has gone into four figures and serves as an effective barrier to the newcomer. The Writers Guild of America has maintained the low initiation fee of fifty dollars, of which only thirty-five must be paid when membership begins. Thus the Guild has maintained what has been called "an open union and a union shop."

CREDITS

Because of the importance of credits to the professional standing of the writer, each of the agreements has detailed provisions on the subject. Each sets up "credit arbitration" machinery in case a writer feels that the credits planned for a program do not correctly describe his contribution.

The television-film agreement states that the company will not

> enter into any contract to give credit to any writer or writers hereunder for reasons of the writer's prestige or for any reasons other than earned credit.

In general, television-film credits are confined to the following possible forms:

> Teleplay by
> Story by
> Written by
>   (meaning story and teleplay by)
> Special material by
>   (for variety shows, etc.)
> Adaptation by

The live-television agreement permits some variants including:

> Written for television by
> Written especially for (name of show) by
> Adapted for television by
> Adapted especially for (name of show) by

The documentary-television agreement permits some additional variants:

> Writer
> Continuity by
>   (for interview or discussion programs)
> Special material by
> Documentary script by

A teleplay is defined as

> the final script with individual scenes, full dialogue or monologue (including narration in connection therewith), and camera setups if required; provided, however, that if the Producer desires any script to consist in part of suggested or indicated dialogue (so that an actor portraying a role may extemporize therefrom) such suggested or indicated dialogue shall be deemed to satisfy the requirement of "full dialogue or monologue."

The company must give *visual* credit "and may if it elects give audio credit as well," in the words of the live-television agreement. All agreements have detailed provisions about the relative position of the writer's credit, size of type, and duration. As a sampling, here are a few details from the live-television agreement:

> If the Producer or the Director of the program receives credit alone in frame (on screen), the Employee shall also receive credit alone in frame (on screen), provided that all writing credits to Employees may be given in the same frame. If roller credits are used, the Company shall set the writing credits in such fashion that when they are centered on the screen, no other credit shall be visible.

On dramatic programs and situation comedy programs the writer's credit shall be

> immediately before or after the most prominent credit to the Producer or Director or, in the case of an adaptation, the most prominent credit to the author of the underlying property.

There are additional variations for other kinds of programs.

The film agreement carries similar clauses and also some that limit the right of the company to place the writer's credit over a background that includes advertising matter.

Behind each of these provisions it is easy to discern a history of past grievances.

Within the Guild, the right to vote on problems relating to television is based on the writer's credits in television.

SUBMISSION OF SCRIPTS

The live-television agreement states:

> In seeking employment under this Agreement, any writer may submit his material to another prospective employer if a bona fide offer of employment has not been made to him by the Company within fifteen (15) days after submission of his material to the Company.

SPECULATIVE WRITING

The various agreements forbid any agreement

> whereby the writer shall write material, payment for which is contingent upon acceptance or approval of the producer.

This wording, from the television-film agreement, is paralleled in the live agreement. The clauses are not intended to limit the writer's right to submit material, but to prevent the company from commissioning material on a conditional basis. In the live agreement the company specifically agrees:

> When the Company employs an Employee, the risk of the Employee's competence shall be assumed by the Company. Failure for any reason to broadcast all or part of the material submitted by the Employee shall not relieve the Company of its obligation to pay the amount contracted for . . . unless the Employee has first breached his contract of employment.

The film agreement, in somewhat different fashion, achieves the same effect.

ATTENDANCE AT REHEARSALS

The live agreement states that the writer

> shall be entitled to attend all writing conferences and rehearsals dealing with material prepared or written by him and the Company shall, upon the Employee's request, inform him in advance of all such conferences and rehearsals . . .

The television-film contract is more equivocal. The company in this agreement recognizes the desirability of the writer's presence at conferences and rehearsals but states that the company has

> the right, in its sole discretion, in any particular case, to determine who will be present at such conferences and rehearsals.

In any event, the writer's discussion is to be

> restricted to material prepared by him, and he shall not carry on such discussions with anyone other than the Producer or director of the program, or their designees.

This applies equally to live television.

REVISIONS

If revisions are needed, says the live-television agreement, the writer shall have

the opportunity to do the first rewrite, unless, after reasonable
efforts to give reasonable notice, he is not available. The Company may require the Employee to do a total of two rewrites,
but not more than two without his consent.

The writer frequently agrees to do more, because otherwise
credits may eventually be shared with another writer.

If a production executive does the rewriting

the rights of the first Employee in said material so rewritten
shall be the same as they would have been if all such rewriting
had been done by the first Employee.

RIGHT TO VIEW FILM

The television-film agreement specifies rules by which the
company must give writers an opportunity to see the "rough
cut" of the film and the final "answer print."

SINGLE USE

The live-television agreement provides that the company, by
means of an employment contract governing a script, obtains
the right to a *single use* of the script, within a specified period
of time. It also acquires *exclusivity*—no other company shall
telecast it during the fifty-two weeks following delivery of the
script. In the case of a script complete in itself, the writer may
make other disposition of the script after the exclusivity period.
In the case of a script written for a series, only the "extricable
elements" may be used by him; he acquires, of course, no rights
in any elements that are part and parcel of the series.

During the period of exclusivity the company may at its
option decide to broadcast the script again, but a fee is paid
for each such rebroadcast.

Failure to broadcast the script within a specified period of
time causes all rights to revert to the writer but does not relieve
the company of financial obligations incurred in the employment
contract. The period is normally 26 weeks but may be much
longer in the case of programs involving higher payments to
the writer.

The single-use restriction does not apply, of course, to television films. Here the agreements provide for continuing use of the film ("forever") by the company, and a schedule of additional remuneration for the writer. The formula for such payments is being restudied jointly by the Guild and the producers.

In the case of a television film the company has *exclusive* television use of the script for five years from the delivery of the script. After that

> Producer and writer shall each have a nonexclusive right to utilize and exploit the film television rights in the material.

In other words, although the company retains the right to use the film and the material in it, the writer too may make use of it.

INCIDENTAL USES

The company acquiring the right to use a script acquires without extra payment various incidental rights. These include, for example, the right to make copies for rehearsal purposes and the right to use material from the script to publicize the program. Another incidental right is the right to have a film print of the program shown at film festivals. In the case of the documentary-television-film agreement, this applies

> even though a nominal admission fee is charged by the festival or competition and provided the Producer derives no profit from such exhibition.

MINIMUM FEES

The agreements include complex schedules of minimum payments. They are complex because they involve special provisions for various categories. In live television, for example, minimums are higher for commercial than for sustaining programs, and higher for originals than for adaptations. There are also special allowances for programs broadcast more than once a week, and special provisions for long-term contracts. There are also special provisions for comedy programs, often written by groups of six, or even eight, writers. The writer should consult one of the Guild offices on the minimum applicable in any particular case.

INCOME FROM SUBSIDIARY USES

The live-television agreement provides that the writer of a one-time program, or of a contribution to a series in which every script is complete in itself, keeps all income from the sale of book, magazine, film, or stage rights unless the sale was made while the company had exclusivity. In that case there is a division, on a scale included in the live-television agreement. The company receives a share of the income because its production is presumed to have contributed to it. The share is larger if there has been a second production, still larger if there has been a third production.

Special formulas are provided for serials and series with continuing characters ("episodic series"). Here the company's share is larger and the company has greater control.

In the television-film contract various nontelevision rights are specifically reserved to the writer, but the company has certain controls over their use, for various periods of time.

COLLABORATION

If two writers collaborate voluntarily, the applicable minimum is the single minimum. A collaboration required by the company is treated differently. The live-television agreement continues:

> No employee shall unreasonably refuse to collaborate with any other Employee assigned by the Company. However . . . the applicable minimums of compensation shall be paid to each employee severally and not jointly.

An important protection is this additional clause:

> Where the Company assigns as collaborator a production executive or supervisory employee, the rights of the first employee in the material shall be the same as they would have been if the writing had been done by the first Employee without such collaboration . . .

The problem of the producer who decides to be a collaborator is an old one, and the Guild has been determined to remove all possible temptation in that direction. An additional deterrent is the following:

> The granting of writing credits to Production Executives shall be subject to the credit arbitration procedure . . .

Selected Readings

Selected Readings

Barnouw, Erik, *Mass Communication: Television, Radio, Film, Press.* New York: Rinehart, 1956.

Barry, Michael, (ed.), *The Television Playwright.* New York: Hill and Wang, 1960.

Britton, Florence, (ed.), *Best Television Plays 1957.* New York: Ballantine Books, 1957.

Burack, A. S., (ed.), *Television Plays for Writers.* Boston: The Writer, Inc., 1957.

Chayefsky, Paddy, *Television Plays.* New York: Simon and Schuster, 1955.

Chester, Giraud, and Garrison, Garnet, *Television and Radio.* New York: Appleton-Century-Crofts, 1956.

Conant, Michael, *Antitrust in the Motion Picture Industry.* Berkeley and Los Angeles: University of California Press, 1960.

Greene, Robert S., *Television Writing, Theory and Technique.* New York: Harper and Brothers, (Rev.) 1956.

Halas, John, and Manvell, Roger, *The Technique of Film Animation.* New York: Hastings House, 1959.

Murrow, Edward R., and Friendly, Fred W., *See It Now.* New York: Simon and Schuster, 1955.

Rose, Reginald, *Six Television Plays.* New York: Simon and Schuster, 1956.

Serling, Rod, *Patterns: Four Television Plays.* New York: Simon and Schuster, 1957.

Settel, Irving, *Best Television Humor.* New York: Ace Books, 1956.

Siepmann, Charles A., *Radio, Television, and Society.* New York: Oxford University Press, 1950.

Stasheff, Edward, and Bretz, Rudy, *The Television Program.* New York: Hill and Wang, (Rev.) 1962.

Vidal, Gore, (ed.), *Best Television Plays.* New York: Ballantine Books, 1956.

Writers Guild of America, *Best Television and Radio Plays of 1956.* New York: Random House, 1957.

Index

ABC-TV, see American Broadcasting Company
Action, 4 ff., 104, 112, 114, 118
Adventure, 136
Adventures of Ozzie and Harriet, The, 126
Advertiser, 26–28, 30, 32, 33, 36, 39, 40–43, 45–46
Advertising agency, 19, 26–29, 31, 41
Age of Kings, An, 140
Agent, 29
American Broadcasting Company, 64
American Civil Liberties Union, 7–8
American Legion, 8
Animation, 11–15, 110, 142, 144, 146
Animation stand, 15
Anthology series, 35, 54
Antitrust, 18, 37, 38
Aquanauts, 42
Armstrong *Circle Theatre,* 8, 27
Audio credit, 164
Author, 16–18

Bachelor Party, 35
Barrow Report, 38–39
Barry, Michael, 114, 140
Batten, Barton, Durstine & Osborn, 27, 28
Bell & Howell, 28
Benny, Jack, 148

Bensfield, Dick, 126
Bergen, Edgar, 148
Best Television Humor, 88, 126, 134, 148
Best Television Plays, 96
Best Television Plays, 1957, 66, 84
BG (background), 94
Bilmar Productions, 154
"Blue Serge Suit," 84
Bob Cummings Show, 88
British Broadcasting Corporation, 102, 140
Britton, Florence, 66
"Bronco," 58, 94
Bundy, McGeorge, 86
Burack, A. S., 5, 62
Burke, Albert, 74
Burns, George, 10

Californians, The, 16
Cameo Playhouse, 86
Camera animation, 13–15
Camera usage, 5, 88–97, 116, 152
Casals Master Class, 35
Catered Affair, A, 35
CBS Reports, 25, 120
CBS–TV, see Columbia Broadcasting System
CBS Workshop, 25
Censorship, 27, 37–38
Center for Mass Communication, 144

Chayefsky, Paddy, 5, 6, 35, 36, 116
Chester, Giraud, 3
Cheyenne, 6, 29, 58, 94
"Christmas Show," 90
Circle Theatre, 8, 27
City of Gold, 14
Clark, Walter van Tilburg, 13
Climax, 4, 66, 154–56
Clinton and the Law, 43
Close-up, 28
Code 3, 42, 108
Collaboration, 169
Collective bargaining, 18, 19, 161
Columbia Broadcasting System, 7, 13, 25, 28, 44, 86, 120, 136
Comedy, 10, 94
Commercials, 11, 28, 62, 110, 142
Communications Act of 1934, 21
Connolly, Joe, 56, 156
Constitution, United States, 11, 16
Contracts, 17, 19, 86, 161
Copyright law, 17
Corwin, Norman, 25
Covered Wagon, The, 15
Credits, 18, 20, 70, 72–77, 102, 163–65
Crime and Punishment, 86
"Cuba: the Battle of America," 74
Cut, 122–26

Davidson, David, 36
"Death Takes an Encore," 100, 112, 118
Dialogue, 9, 15, 118
Dialogue and action, 104–15
Dialogue perspective, 98–103
"Die by the Gun," 132
Directions 61, 64
Disney, Walt, 11
Dissolve, 102, 128

Documentary, 8, 12, 13, 102, 106
Doud, Earle, 92, 150
Dragnet, 8, 9, 118
Drama, 5 ff., 9, 15–16, 45, 70
Durante, Jimmy, 10
Durfee, Hazard, 13, 14

Eggers, Fred, 54
Elizabethan drama, 4
Elward, James, 78
Employee status, 17–20, 25, 29, 161 ff.
Employers, 21 ff., 29, 31 ff., 35
Eternal Light, The, 34
Exclusivity, 167
Explorer, The, 66
Exposition, 5, 62
Exterior, 56

Fade-out, fade-in, 130
"Family on Trial," 108
Father Knows Best, 92
Federal Communications Commission, 21–22, 30, 36, 38–39
FG (foreground), 94
Flaherty, Robert, 10
Fletcher, John, 7
Flintstones, The, 12, 13
Foote, Horton, 35, 36
Ford Foundation, 29, 34
Foshko, Robert, 92
Four Star Films, Inc., 132
Freedom of the press, 39, 40
Friendly, Fred W., 7, 43
Funday Funnies, 29
Garrison, Garnet, 3
Gilroy, Frank, 84
Gomalco Productions, Inc., 56, 156
Goodyear *Playhouse,* 5, 6, 30, 35
Grant, Perry, 126
Grapes of Wrath, The, 15
Graphic material, 134, 138–47

Griffith, D. W., 36
Guild shop, 163

Halas, John, 110
Harbor Command, 42
Harvey Comics, Inc., 29
Hawaiian Eye, 6, 16, 42
Henning, Paul, 88
"He Shall Have Power," 86
Hill, George Roy, 68
Historical footage, 14
Hong Kong, 6, 16, 42
Honor, 130
Hook, 13, 14
Hoover, Herbert, 40
Hope, Bob, 10
Hosts, 9
Howard, Bob, 134

Ibsen, 5, 6, 10, 45
"Incident on the Edge of Madness," 60
Incidental uses, 168
Independent contractor, 18 ff.
Independent producer, 26–31, 36, 38, 45
Indianapolis, Indiana, 7
Industrialization of the writer, 16–18
Initiation fees, union, 163
Interior, 56

Jack Paar Show, 134, 150
"Jewish Perspective, A," 64
Jewish Theological Seminary of America, 34, 64
Johnny Midnight, 16, 42
Journalism, 6 ff., 45

Kane, Frank, 100, 112
"Kathy Wins an Oscar," 92
Kelland, C. B., 58
"King's Ransom," 128
Kinoy, Ernest, 52
Kneale, Nigel, 140

Knopf, Christopher, 132
Kraft Playhouse, 26

Langdon, John, 84
Lassie, 6
Lawrence, Jerome, 25
Leave It to Beaver, 56, 156
Lee, James, 86
Lee, Robert E., 25
Lewis, Shari, 90
Library footage, 132
Licensing, 21–25
Limbo, 84, 86
Lineup, The, 54
Liss, Abe, 13
Little, Herbert, Jr., 60
Lord, Walter, 68

Macgowan, Kenneth, 9
MacLeish, Archibald, 25
Magazine concept, 45
Malcolm Productions, Inc., 132
Malibu Run, 16
Man on the Mountaintop, 96
Manvell, Roger, 110
Marks, Larry, 134
Marty, 35
Matter of Pride, A, 84
McCarthy, Charlie, 148
Meet McGraw, 128
Meet the Press, 33
Menkin, Lawrence, 108, 132
Men of Annapolis, 156
Metropolitan Broadcasting Company, 74
Mickey Spillane Series, 100, 112
Minimum basic agreement, 162
Miracle Worker, The, 35
Mitchell, Denis, 102
M. M. Inc., 128
Models, 134
Morris, Colin, 114
Moser, James, 154
Mosher, Robert, 56, 156
Motion Picture Patents Company, 37

Mrs. Wickens in the Fall, 140
M Squad, 16
Murrow, Edward R., 7, 43, 120
Museum of Natural History, 136
Music, 15, 150–52
Mutual Broadcasting System, 23

Naked City, 16, 42
Narration, 8–11, 15, 68, 70, 84, 86, 116–21, 146
National Association of Broadcasters, 40
National Broadcasting Company, 10, 14, 15, 45, 90, 146, 152
National Educational Television and Radio Center, 34, 144
National Labor Relations Act, 18
NBC–TV, see National Broadcasting Company
Nelson, Don, 126
Nelson, Ozzie, 126
NET, see National Educational Television and Radio Center
Networks, 19, 22–26, 29–33, 38–39, 41, 43, 44, 45
Night to Remember, A, 68–71
Noon on Doomsday, 28
Nuremberg Trials, The, 27

Off-screen narration, 8, 15, 74, 116, 118, 120
O'Hanlon, James, 58
Old MacDonald Had a Curve, 122–25, 138
Omnibus, 11, 29, 86
O'Neill, Eugene, 45
Opening, 62–71
Option, network, 23, 32

Paar, Jack, 134, 150
Pan-American Airways, 44
Paper Foxhole, 78, 104
Patterns, 35, 82

Patterns: Four Television Plays, 82, 122
Philco-Goodyear *Playhouse,* 5, 6, 30, 35
Philip Marlowe, 154
Piel Brothers, 12
Playhouse 90, 6, 30, 42
Playhouse Pictures, Inc., 110
Play of the Week, 21, 33
Portrait of Lincoln, 14
Primer of Playwriting, 9
Printer's Measure, 116
Prize Plays of Television and Radio, 1956, 68, 78
Process shot, 132
Public interest, convenience, and necessity, 22
Public service agency, 34–35
Pursuit, 108

Racket Squad, 42
Radio Act of 1927, 21
Ratings, 8
Rawhide, 60, 80
Real Case of Murder, A, 120
Real West, The, 14, 15, 146
Rear projection, 132–35
Rehearsal, 166
Reisman, Philip, Jr., 14, 146
Requiem for a Heavyweight, 35
Rescue 8, 16
Return Engagement, 112
Revisions, 19, 20, 165
Revue Productions, Inc., 100, 112
Reznick, Sidney, 134
Robert Saudek Associates, 86
Rodgers, Richard, 14
Rodman, Howard, 67
Roller credits, 165
Rose, Reginald, 5, 35, 62, 72
Rough Riders, 42

"Samuel McCutcheon Case, The," 54
See It Now, 8, 30

Sergeant Dekker, 16
Serling, Rod, 28, 82
Settel, Irving, 88
Setting, 5, 78–87
Shakespeare, William, 4, 6, 9, 10, 140
Shari Lewis Show, 90
Shaw, G. B., 45
Sheena, Queen of the Jungle, 32
Sherwood, Robert, 45
Shot, the, 94, 96, 118
Shriner, Herb, 10
Shuken, Phil, 88
Sommers, Jay, 126
Sophocles, 10
Sound effects, 106, 108, 122, 148, 150–53
Sound and Music, 150–53
Speculative writing, 165–66
Sponsor, 26–28, 32, 33, 36
Standard Oil of New Jersey, 34
Stapp, Philip, 144
Star, 31, 36
Station, 21 ff., 30
Stills, 134, 138, 146
Stock footage, 58, 128, 132
Story board, 110
Story of a Family, The, 10
Strindberg, August, 45
Submission of scripts, 50 ff., 165
Subsidiary uses, 169
Super Circus, 76
Supreme Court, United States, 37, 44
Surinach, Carlos, 13
Syndicates, 21, 31–33, 39–40

Talent Associates, 27
Tarcher Productions, 90
Teaser, 62
Teacher, 10–11
"Teatime," 110
Techniques of Film Animation, The, 110
Television Plays, 116
Television Plays for Writers, 130

Television Playwright, The, 114, 116
Telop, 138
Tenth Man, The, 35
Theatre Guild, Inc., 28
Thompson, J. Walter, Inc., 26
Thornley, Steven, 128
Time, 12, 23, 124, 126, 128, 130
Time, Inc., 28
Title pages, 52–61
Tombstone Territory, 16
Trackdown, 16
Tragedy in a Temporary Town, 62, 72, 98
Transition, 122–31
Trucking shot, 110
Turteltaub, Saul, 90
TV Guide, 54
Twelve Angry Men, 35
Twentieth Century, 25, 30

United Artists Corporation, 32
United Nations, 144
United States *v.* Paramount *et al.,* 37, 39
Unloved, The, 114
U. S. Steel Hour, 28

Venice Film Festival, 35
Victor, David, 60
Victory At Sea, 14, 25, 30, 33
Vidal, Gore, 5, 35, 36, 96, 130
Videotape recording, 6
Violence, 112
Visit to a Small Planet, 35
Visual credit, 164
Visual writing, 114, 144
Voice-over narration, 116

Wagon Train, 16, 42
Walk Down the Hill, A, 52
Wanted—Dead or Alive, 16, 42, 132
Warner Brothers, 29, 58
Water, 144

Way of Thinking, A, 74
Weaver, Sylvester, 45
Welles, Orson, 25
What in the World?, 34
Whedon, John, 68
Wide, Wide World, 30, 150

Wind of Change, The, 102, 106
Wishengrad, Morton, 34, 36, 64
Writers Guild of America, 7, 19,
   20, 36, 161 ff.

Ziv-United Artists, 32

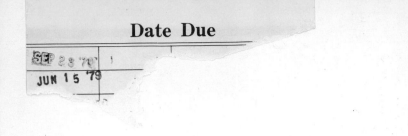